In this remarkable book, my good friend Joe Stowell puts Christ and our relationship with him back at the center of Christianity, where it belongs. This book is "must reading" for those who are tired of plastic religion and who wish to pursue an authentic faith.

Dr. Tony Evans, Oak Cliff Bible Fellowship, Dallas

Bringing a remarkable blend of simplicity with sublimity, Joe draws the heart of the reader into the greatest pursuit of life—following Christ. This book will join the ranks of those that are not just read but lived out.

Ravi Zacharias, Ravi Zacharias International Ministries

In *Following Christ,* Joe Stowell has washed away the graffiti of our own agendas, activities, and attitudes, revealing what it truly means to be a disciple. For those who are dissatisfied with mediocrity and bored with religiosity, this book is a must.

Anne Graham Lotz, Author and Conference Speaker

I often assess the value of a Christian book by whether it leaves me feeling closer to the One I love. By that standard, this book is pure gold.

Bill Hybels, Senior Pastor, Willow Creek Community Church

FOLLOWING CHRIST

CHRIST

EXPERIENCING LIFE

THE WAY IT WAS

MEANT TO BE

Joseph M. Stowell

ZondervanPublishingHouse

Grand Rapids, Michigan

A Division of HarperCollinsPublishers

ZONDERVAN™

Following Christ
Copyright © 1996 by Joseph M. Stowell

Requests for information should be addressed to:
Zondervan, *Grand Rapids, Michigan 49530*

Library of Congress Cataloging-in-Publication Data

Stowell, Joseph M.
    Following Christ : experiencing life the way it was meant to be / Joseph M.
Stowell.
       p. cm.
    Includes bibliographical references.
    ISBN 0-310-21934-5 (Softcover)
    1. Christian life.   2. Jesus Christ—Lordship.   I. Title.
BV4501.2.S7944 1996
248.4—dc20
                                       96-19718
                                          CIP

Permissions and credits are acknowledged in the Notes, pages 221–23, which hereby
become part of this copyright page.

Interior design by Sue Vandenberg Koppenol

Printed in the United States of America

        08 09 /❖ DC/   15 16 17 18 19 20

To
Joy, Rod, and Debbie,
who married our children and have
brought an expanded sense of joy and
delight to our family

CONTENTS

PREFACE

Of all the mental disorders, hearing voices is perhaps the most unsettling. Yet it seems that our lives are rendered dysfunctional by all the real voices we hear trying to direct, counsel, and control life. From the time we were kids we have heard voices telling us to do this and to do that, to go here and not to go there, this is important and that is not. Growing up doesn't solve the problem—it only makes it worse. During adolescence, the voices of our peers often conflict with the parental voices heard at home. Then there are the religious voices, professors' voices, trendy voices, voices from the media and entertainment, and even voices from within that leave us dizzy with a cacophony of contradictory input and advice.

Life is a search for a voice we can trust—a single voice that puts all other voices into quiet perspective, a voice that settles the loudness around us and speaks peacefully yet clearly and confidently.

A voice that we can gladly follow.

Jesus Christ is the Voice. He affirmed, "My sheep listen to my voice; I know them, and they follow me" (John 10:27).

Those who have set their hearts to hear His voice and follow have been liberated from the din and frustration of the seductive voices that threaten their destinies.

Unfortunately, to look at most of us who call ourselves by His name, it would be hard to tell that we hear His voice alone and follow it. Our lives are more often than not dictated by our "want-to" voices within and by the most pressing and influential voices around us.

This book is about freeing ourselves from the voices that haunt us. It is about the primary pursuit and the most privileged identity of life. It is about becoming what God intended us to be. It is about experiencing life the way it was meant to be.

Following Christ leads us to embrace and experience the primal call of our Christianity as we learn both what it means to become fully devoted followers of Him and how we can actualize that desire.

The following pages flow out of Christ's call to His first followers, "Follow me . . . and I will make you fishers of men" (Matt. 4:19). This expanded exposition of the call develops . . .

. . . an awareness of the issues that make followership such a challenging endeavor;

. . . a realistic appraisal of the lesser voices in our lives that call us down different and sometimes destructive paths;

. . . the specific meaning of the call to follow, applied in the context of life in a fallen yet alluring world;

. . . the compelling nature of the Person who calls and the ways to developing increasing intimacy with Him;

. . . the nature of the cause that He will lead us to;

. . . the nets that stand in the way of experiencing life in the way with Him;

. . . the inevitable yet glorious reality of picking up our cross and following Him.

Relating successfully to Christ begins by relating to Him as followers. He doesn't relate to us on any other turf. Yet we hear little about following. For most of us, Christianity has been formed in paradigms of a system in which earthly leadership is paramount. We are led to believe that if we relate successfully to the structure, we are doing well in our Christianity—especially if we serve well enough to become leaders. If we have heard about following at all, it is usually in terms of earthly persons, codes, and institutions. Christianity has become more of a ritual and less of a relationship, more of a system and less of a Savior who like a shepherd leads us.

Followers know that Christianity is different. They know that it is Christ and Christ alone. Fully devoted followers experience the liberating joy of simplifying their lives by simply following Christ.

Followers never say to themselves, "I think I'll make something of my life! And, oh yes, I'll try to follow Him as well." Instead, they readily and happily embrace the reality that Christ said, "Follow Me and let *Me* make something of your life."

Those who rise to the Voice and set their hearts and minds on becoming non-negotiated, uncompromised followers begin the marvelous adventure of experiencing life the way it was meant to be.

WITHOUT THEM...

As our Lord uses this book to clarify His call in your life, thank...

... Him. He is the one who called us to follow. These pages are just an expression of His primary intention for our lives.

... those who have researched this call and processed it in their lives. I am indebted to their writings and observations.

... Beth Longjohn, whose tirelessly creative work in the processing of the manuscript and the research of key illustrations and texts was invaluable in guaranteeing the accuracy and effectiveness of this project. Beth, I will be forever grateful.

... Lori Imhof, whose efficient work as my secretary frees me to the ministry of writing. Lori, your capacity to move through the myriad of the stress and stuff with such grace and maturity both amazes and encourages me.

... Kent Hughes, Bill Hendricks, and Gary Chapman, who graciously supplied solid supportive material.

... Billie Sue Thompson, Ray Carter, and Greg Thornton, whose suggestions on the manuscript were critical in the early stages. and...

... the great team at Zondervan whose editorial support and helpful advice as the project matured provided an indispensable ingredient in the formation of the material. Hats off to Stan Gundry, Jack Kuhatschek, Jim Ruark, and John Topliff.

As Jesus was walking beside the Sea of Galilee, he saw two brothers, Simon called Peter and his brother Andrew. They were casting a net into the lake, for they were fishermen. "Come, follow me," Jesus said, "and I will make you fishers of men." At once they left their nets and followed him.

Going on from there, he saw two other brothers, James son of Zebedee and his brother John. They were in a boat with their father Zebedee, preparing their nets. Jesus called them, and immediately they left the boat and their father and followed him.

(Matt. 4:18–22)

CHAPTER ONE

FOLLOW THE LEADER

High Stakes in the Game Called Life

Gandhi was asked by a close friend, "If you admire Christ so much, why don't you become a Christian?" Gandhi reportedly replied, "When I meet a Christian who is a follower of Christ, I may consider it."

Mao Tse-tung came to America as a university student, intrigued by Christianity and Western culture. But after encountering several Christians and our brand of Christianity, he became disillusioned and turned his heart toward Marxism. We all know the rest of the story.

It seems to me that this is not what Christ had in mind when He said, "Follow Me, and I will make you fishers of men."

Something significant has happened since Christ issued that call nearly two thousand years ago. We have become quite happy to call ourselves Christians with little or no thought of following. As a result, we are paying dearly through a loss of fulfillment, personal satisfaction, and our impact on our world.

It is not that we have denied Christ or even that we have done horrible things. In fact, most of us have mastered the codes of conduct and rituals of our religion. The problem is, we have masqueraded Christ with our own ways. When non-Christians see us, they see more of our distorted portrayal of Christianity than they do a clear reflection of the character and quality of Christ.

During the rush and crush of the past Christmas season, I wandered into a store only to be greeted by the stern stare of the clerk, who said in cold, unwelcoming terms, "We are closed."

To which I naively replied, "Well, the door was open!"

Her response was chillier than before. "I said, we're closed."

When non-Christians see us, they see more of our
distorted portrayal of Christianity than they do a
clear reflection of the character and quality of Christ.

It wasn't the fact that they were closed that triggered my response. It was her uncaring, rejecting attitude that prompted me to mutter, "Don't be rude."

I turned back toward the revolving door through which I had entered and pushed on it to leave. As I did so, she said, loud enough for others to hear, "You're pushing it the wrong way! Do you want to break our door?"

I pushed it the other way, and it seemed to be locked. So I asked her, "How can I push it the other way? It's locked."

She replied, "It's not locked." And then in an obvious affront to my maleness, she said to the few people gathered at the cash register, "Will someone please help this man with the door?"

I pushed a little harder, and it moved in the right direction, while my ego lay in pieces on the floor.

As I drove home, the scenario nagged my mind and heart. I wished that I had not replied so stubbornly and caustically with words that contradicted her claim to be closed. My retort about her being rude only incited her already acrimonious spirit. She had proved to be more than a match for me, and I deeply regretted getting into a confrontation.

But what I regretted more was the fact that I had failed to show her the reality of the living Christ through my words and attitude. I was haunted by the thought that someone in that cash register line might have known that I was from Moody Bible Institute. More troubling was the prospect that they might tell the clerk. It is not the reputation of Moody that concerns me—it is that in people's minds Moody connects me to Christ. They saw me at my worst that night, and if they knew who I was, they could have concluded, "If this is what Christ means in a person's life, then forget it."

It is one thing to damage our own reputations. It is quite another to deface and defame Christ—especially since in His pure form He is intriguingly attractive.

Living in Chicago, I am aware of what graffiti can do to an otherwise attractive façade. Throughout history, vandals have destroyed masterpieces of art by wanton strokes of a brush, adding glasses, a mustache, a sinister smile, a beard, or a distorted nose.

Too often we have graffitied the face of Christ. His image becomes clouded by our prejudices and preferences. Apart from our activities on Sunday and our conformity to external codes of dos and don'ts, the world doesn't notice much difference between us and people who don't claim to be Christians. All they see in Christianity is the loss of a day of leisure on the weekend and the denial of common pleasures. Nor does it go unnoticed that many professing Christians manifest as much greed, self-centeredness, materialism, anger, aggressiveness, and sensualism as the average pagan on the street.

Our record on issues that relate to racial prejudice and cross-cultural sensitivity is especially poor. While we rightly lift a prophetic voice against moral ills such as abortion and homosexual behavior, we are strangely silent on issues that touched the heart of Christ—the poor, oppression, and injustice.

Few will be drawn to Christianity as a system, especially in its graffitied form. Yet those who find their way through the distortion discover Christ as a compelling draw.

MIRRORS IN MOTION

Fully devoted followers are like mirrors in motion. By the very definition of following, we are called into a deepening intimacy with Christ. This increasingly close proximity to Christ transforms us and results in a clear reflection of His character. As followers we replicate the grace, mercy, love, justice, compassion, truth, and righteousness of Christ our leader. Followers refuse to be satisfied just to be saved and on their way to heaven. For followers, Christianity is a relationship, an adventure, a passionate pursuit of Christ. Followers escape the boredom and drudgery of a system of rituals and regulations and revel in the discovery of this intriguing Person.

Following is the beginning and the end of what it means to be a Christian. Everything in between is measured by it.

As followers we are liberated from religious traditions and conventions that do not reflect the perspective, character, and conduct of Christ. Although we may hear a multiplicity of voices from both within and outside the church, we listen to only one. It is the voice of Christ, who simply said, "Follow Me." No conditions. No negotiations. No particulars. No contractual exceptions. Just follow. It was the first and last thing Jesus said to Peter (Mark 1:17; John 21:19, 22). It is the beginning and the end of what it means to be a Christian. Everything in between is measured by it.

Followers are free—free to be what they were intended to be, free to experience life the way it was meant to be.

Unfortunately, we don't readily perceive ourselves as followers. When we identify ourselves, it is most often with terms such as "Christian," "believer," "brother," or "sister." To say, "I am a Christian," focuses our attention on our privileges and entitlements. Or, perhaps it is simply a way to differentiate ourselves from other kinds of people. For some it means little more than not being a Muslim, Hindu, or Buddhist. The title itself does little to forge a sense of calling, action, or definition of what being a Christian is all about. Some of us have understood the vagueness of the title "Christian" and have opted for "believer." But this only focuses on a time or season when we confirmed the fact that we had chosen to believe in Christ and His gospel. Again, this fails to define or delineate what it actually means to live as a believer. What does a believer do apart from giving mental assent to a system of belief? Then there is the identity of "brother" or "sister." The problem here is that these terms focus our attention horizontally, in terms of relationships to one another, not primarily on our relationship to Christ.

Others of us think of our relationship with Christ in terms of "I am a Baptist" or Lutheran, Presbyterian, Methodist, or some other denominational or group label.

As good and important as these identities may be, at some point we have to get beyond these labels to a self-perception that will demand the right stuff of our lifestyle. Identifying ourselves as followers captures the essence of what it means to be a believing Christian. Think of the difference it would make if we answered questions about who we are by saying, "I am a follower of Christ." Calling one another "follower" would draw out both encouragment and accountability. Thinking of ourselves as followers keeps our focus on Christ and holds us accountable for how we live.

Yet, in a strange, twisted sort of way, many of us live out our faith in Christ as though He exists to follow us. We come to believe that Christ exists to satisfy our demands. Distorted perceptions of Christianity pose the power of faith and prayer as instruments designed to get Christ to serve our impulses for peace and prosperity. This disguised form of self-serving religion sets Christ up as just one more commodity in life that will enhance and empower our dreams and destinations.

An informed perspective of following cancels that notion. Of course, Christ wishes to grant good things to us because He *is* generous. But He gives us good things out of His pleasure, in His time and His way, not out of any authority that we supposedly have over Him. F. B. Meyer writes of the free flowing generosity of our Father:

> Now and again there is a *dash of extra sweetness* poured into life's cup—some special deliverance; some unlooked-for interposition; some undeserved and unusual benediction—sent apparently for no other object than to satisfy God's passion for giving. . . .
>
> With Him, the calf is always the fatted calf; the robe is always the best robe; the joy is unspeakable; the peace passeth understanding; the grace is so abundant that the recipient has all-sufficiency for all things, and abounds in every good work. There is no grudging in God's benevolence.[1]

It is this good and generous Christ who rises on the landscape of life as our compelling, all-consuming reality and calls us to follow Him.

Wherever.

Whatever.

We must not forget that all of life suffers when we fail to follow. We were created to follow. In the very beginning, God created us in His image so that we could connect with Him as our transcendent guide who would lead us to the reality of the life He desires for us. But if we have chosen life on our own terms, we become disillusioned, wondering why life is not all it's cracked up to be.

ACCEPTING THE CHALLENGE

It is not that we have not heard that intriguing call, "Follow Me." It is not even that we do not believe in and admire the One who calls. Our struggle is that it is just plain difficult to be a follower. In a world consumed with leadership, independence, and self-led living, it is tough to find volunteers who will even admit that they want to be followers. We get and give the impression that followers are limp, vulnerable, weak, controlled by others, and lacking in initiative.

Robert Kelley, whose book *The Power of Followership* deals with the strategic value of being a follower, relates,

> In the years since I began researching this book, I have had the following conversation many times. A friend, a stranger sitting next to me on a plane, an executive, or a journalist will ask, "What are you working on?"
> "Followership," I say.
> "What? Run that by me again."
> "Followership, the flip side of leadership," I explain.
> "Oh, you mean the people who need to be told what to do. The sheep?"[2]

I don't know whether kids still play Follow the Leader, but I can remember spending some of my wasted youth in the pursuit. Interestingly, I always wanted to be the leader. In fact, so did just about everyone else. The reason? The leader was always right, never caught off guard, and never embarrassed by having to imitate others. It is like playing Simon Sez: The leader always looks good, and the followers are the ones who stumble and can't quite keep up.

Growing up hasn't changed our perception
of the difference between leading and following—
only now it's not a game, and the stakes are high.

Growing up hasn't changed our perception of the difference between leading and following—only now it's not a game, and the stakes are high. All of life and its outcomes rise and fall on whether or not we will choose to be the leader of our own destiny or a follower of someone wiser and better fit to lead. Unfortunately, when it comes to the life choices that matter most, we resist yielding control. We don't want to give the impression that we are unable to figure out life for ourselves. Like men who refuse to stop and ask directions when they are lost, we fear that others will think we aren't wise and strong.

Or perhaps it's just our "want-tos" that lead us astray.

In the face of our resistance to being vulnerable, Christ calls us to come after Him. He calls us to count ourselves singularly, wholly, and without compromise fully devoted followers of Him—not as a part-time expression of, or add-on to, our Christianity, but as the all-consuming center point of our existence. Yet this tension between the call of Christ and our resistance to following puts the experience and expression of authentic Christianity in jeopardy.

Rick, surrounded by 64,000 other men, sat in the Dome Stadium in Minneapolis and listened as the speaker spoke pointedly about personal purity. At the close of the message, thousands of the men stood to commit and recommit themselves to lives of integrity and moral purity. Rick knew that this kind of commitment would mean not going over to Vicki's apartment on weekends. It would mean denying a part of his life that he had come to both enjoy and count on. As he watched other men stand, he remembered how convincing his university professor had been in claiming that there are no moral absolutes. When another Christian in the class disagreed, the professor systematically dismantled the student's point of view. There was no doubt that few in the class held any sympathy for those who believe that some things are always right and some always wrong. Now, sitting in that stadium and troubled in mind, Rick wondered why he should give up his relationship with Vicki. Maybe these guys are just being manipulated into a religious experience by the power of the moment and the compelling presentation of the speaker. Rick never stood. Rick didn't follow.

MaryAnne's husband had been living for several months in the duplicity of an affair when she found a note folded up into a tiny square in the back pocket of his jeans. When she confronted him, he callously admitted that it was true. He promised never to do it again, yet in the weeks to follow he continued to see the other woman.

At the hairdresser's, MaryAnne read an article that encouraged couples to be free enough to love beyond the scope of their own marriage. The article commented that some affairs can help communication in a marriage and help a couple understand each other better. One anecdote told of a woman who found that having an affair was a satisfying way to even the score with an unfaithful husband. MaryAnne thought of her high-school boyfriend, who still lived in town. Periodically she would run into him, and it was clear that he still had some feelings for her.

Several of MaryAnne's friends at church told her that if they were in her shoes, they would have kicked her husband out a long time ago. Amid the pain of being rejected and betrayed by her husband, she felt torn from without and within. Yet she knew that Christ would want her to honor her promises and would offer mercy, grace, and forgiveness toward her husband. It was clear to her what she must do if she would follow Christ.

Gregory sat in his usual chair at the Tuesday night Bible study at the McCulloughs' home. Tonight, as Bob led the Bible study, it became clear to Gregory that the deal that he and his partner were designing was built on an unethical premise. Few, if any, would ever know. He didn't hear much of what was said for the next several minutes in the Bible study. He knew how badly his wife wanted a special vacation to the Caribbean and how she hoped that this winter she could finally have a fur coat like her friends. The deal would help those dreams come true. His partner also claimed to be a Christian and was, in fact, an elder at a different church from Gregory's. He wouldn't want to hear that this deal was out of bounds. Gregory remembered hearing him dismiss Christians who couldn't buck up and be "good" businessmen. Yet Gregory knew that if he was to be a non-negotiated follower of Christ, he would have to tell his partner in the morning that the deal was off.

CHRISTIANITY IS CHRIST

The struggles that put followership in jeopardy are not uncommon. Yet at the core of it all, it is not a struggle with rules and regulations. The issue is something far more significant, more compelling. Following Christ is a relationship that drives and defines all we are and do. In fact, that's what I love about followership. It's not a project. It's a Person. It's a relationship to a Person who perfectly loves and cares for us and who is wise beyond comparison—a Person who has done so much for His followers that they look for ways to please and obey Him.

> *If Christianity is dull and boring, if it is a burden
> and not a blessing, then most likely we are involved
> in a project, not a Person—a system not a Savior,
> rules rather than a relationship.*

Followership would be drudgery and dull if it were nothing but an obligation to fulfill or a list of rules to keep. We don't find joy and fulfillment in a good marriage because of the institution of marriage, the laws that govern it, or the tax breaks for filing jointly. What would motivate me to change diapers, pick up my clothes, endure crowded aisles in the grocery store, or be faithful? It is relationship. Doing these things for Martie is what gives meaning to the menial tasks of marriage.

If Christianity is dull and boring, if it is a burden and not a blessing, then most likely we are involved in a project, not a Person—a system not a Savior, rules rather than a relationship.

Followership is not a religious thing, a list of rules, a host of rituals, a philosophy of life, or the best choice among other possible lifestyles.

Authentic followers do not live for liturgy or liberation. Following is not celebration. It is not contemporary or traditional. It is not jubilant dance or compelling drama. It is not preaching. It is not praising. It is not obeying or conforming.

It is Christ, and Christ alone.

All the rest is because of Christ and for Christ.

We are prone to embrace the forms and functions as though they were the essence. But they are only the expressions; He is the essence.

Dietrich Bonhoeffer wrote,

> Discipleship means adherence to Christ. . . . An abstract Christology, a doctrinal system, a general religious knowledge on the subject of grace or on the forgiveness of sins, render discipleship superfluous. . . . Christianity without the living Christ is inevitably Christianity without discipleship, and Christianity without discipleship is always Christianity without Christ."[3]

A PASSIONATE PURSUIT

When Christ said, "Follow Me" (Matt. 4:19), He used a specific word that underscores that followers are to embrace Him as the essence of their existence. The word literally means to "come after." Following is a directional thing. It is to position Christ as our singular, passionate pursuit in all things. With every thought, choice, and response to life, fully devoted followers move toward proximity and intimacy with Christ.

Paul Hiebert, professor of missions at Trinity Evangelical Divinity School, envisions biblical Christianity as a paradigm with Christ at the center. He notes that authentic followers are in the process of moving closer to Christ. Each decision moves the arrow closer to the One we are pursuing. Hiebert notes that some who have been moving toward Christ become distracted by some seduction, turn their arrows around, and with wrong choices grow increasingly distant from Christ. And what of us who have decided that we are close enough and simply go into orbit around Christ? This holding pattern is particularly comfortable when we note that others are orbiting farther away than we are. But to be a follower means that Christ is the all-consuming center of our experience toward whom we are moving.

Unfortunately, Hiebert notes, we have often viewed Christianity as open space defined by boundaries of rules, traditions, and doctrine. As long as we stay in the space without climbing over the walls that define Christianity, we assume that we are good Christians. And while it is true that authentic Christianity has well-defined boundaries, authentic Christians do more than compliantly fill space. Christianity is more than a random racquetball experience of bouncing off walls as we are propelled through sanctified air by often conflicting influences that try to direct our Christian experience.

Christianity is Christ at the center, with followers converging steadily toward Him within the context of legitimate biblical boundaries.

Life is like a galaxy. There is always something at the center that defines and directs everything else that moves around it. As the sun is to our solar system, so the Son should be to our existence.

Life is like a galaxy. There is always something at the center that defines and directs everything else that moves around it. As the sun is to our solar system, so the Son should be to our existence. He is the center point that brings light, life, meaning, purpose, and direction to all we do. As the center, He defines and establishes our view of every possession and pursuit.

For many Christians, Christ is relegated to one of the tracks circling whatever it is that we have substituted for Him in the center. Whether it's our career, our plans and dreams, money, friends, self, or a dozen other things, Christ-followers refuse to have anything in the center but Him. Our lives spiral ever closer to Him in tracks of intimacy and fellowship. The closer we get to Him as the center of our universe, the more of Him we reflect. The closer we track, the more of His justice, love, truth, patience, humility, and power is evident in our daily routine.

While true followers acknowledge Christ as the strategic center, most of us stop short of that. We are quite satisfied to relate to Him; accept His liberation from hell; praise Him; find comfort, solace, and joy in Him; and be intrigued by Him. But few are bent toward following Him unconditionally. And that makes all the difference in the world—in our own little world and the larger world around us.

INCREDIBLE IMPACT

Early Christians knew little else but that they were followers. There were no electric guitars or dazzling experiences. Their Christian journey was just following—following that often cost them family, career, and even their lives. Yet their impact was incredible, and it wasn't because they were persons of power and influence. In the early generations of the church, as it is today, most of the followers of Christ were just common folk, not the well-connected elite with access to the power brokers and shakers and movers. Their power and influence would be wielded in a far more strategic venue: the hearts and minds of a watching world. As persecution mounted against them from the political and religious establishments, they were unintimidated and unmoved as followers of Christ. Some died in the arena as fodder for hungry lions; others were covered with pitch and were set on fire as human torches to light the streets of Rome. The reality of a Christ worth living for—dying for if necessary—stirred the curiosity of their world.

The lifestyle of these followers was dramatically and productively different from the people around them. They loved and cared for one another. They cared for their enemies, even the worst of them. They were selfless, sharing with each other and those in need. Politically and economically disenfranchised, they had hope and trust in a transcendent reality that left them strong in the face of poverty and persecution.

Polycarp, a bishop in the Asian city of Smyrna, faced certain death when, during the public games in February A.D. 155, the large, excited crowds began to rally against him. "Away with the atheists!" they shouted, "Let Polycarp be searched for!" His whereabouts betrayed by a tortured young girl, the police came for him. Yet not even the police captain wished to see him die. On the brief journey back to the city, the captain pleaded with the old man, "What harm is it to say, 'Caesar is Lord' and to offer sacrifice and to be saved?"

When Polycarp was brought to the arena, the proconsul gave him the choice of death or cursing the name of Christ and making sacrifice to Caesar. The bishop's response was that of a fully devoted follower: "Eighty and six years have I served Him, and He has done me no wrong. How can I blaspheme my King who saved me?" Threatened with burning, Polycarp then helped put things in perspective for his enemies: "You threaten me with the fire that burns for a time, and is quickly quenched, for you do not know the fire which awaits the wicked in the judgment to come and in everlasting punishment." In spite of the appeals of his persecutors, he remained immovable and was bound to the stake and set afire.

In life, Polycarp's greatest pursuit had been Christ, even to the point of death. As the flames rose around him, he prayed his final prayer: "I bless Thee that Thou hast granted unto me this day and hour, that I may share, among the number of the martyrs, in the cup of Thy Christ, for the resurrection to eternal life."[4]

When asked why they were different, these early Christians testified that they were followers of the man called Christ, who gave them something so wonderful that they would never consider an alternative. Their impact was so powerful that in the fourth century the emperor Constantine recanted of his opposition and embraced Christianity, declaring it the official religion of the Roman Empire.

From that time on, the entire Western culture was shaped and formed for centuries by the power of fully devoted followers. Until just recently, our laws, art, literature, music, and mores all bore the imprint of the foundation that these followers laid.

Their legacy calls to us.

Yet, as we embark on our journey as followers of Christ, we inevitably feel insecure and vulnerable, naked and out of control. Following is always filled with a sense of uncertainty. Even so, getting to know Him as He really is proves that He is eminently worth following.

Followers come to know Him as One to whom we can trustingly submit. We find that any risk in the process of following Christ is well worth the reward. Over the last two thousand years millions have followed Him, and no one has ever ultimately been disappointed.

A SIMPLY WONDERFUL LIFE

One of the rewards of following Christ is the simplicity and wonder it brings to life. The life of a follower is not simple in terms of stress and challenge or wonderful in terms of a rose-strewn pathway. It is simply wonderful in deeper, more enduring ways.

The follower's journey is simple in the sense that the complexity of life is reduced to the single question, "Where is Christ on this issue?" Or put another way, "Am I on the road with Him?" While all the world loses itself in speculation and experimentation about the meaning of life, the follower has a certain and singular focus: Christ. Wherever He is, that is where the follower will be. Wherever He goes, that is the undaunted direction of a follower's life. Followers laugh with Him and cry with Him. They love what He loves and hate what He hates. Amid the tensions of a dozen voices telling us what to do and how to live, His is the one voice that captures the attention of our hearts.

One of the rewards of following Christ is
the simplicity and wonder it brings to life.

Regardless of how tough it is at home, followers do what Christ would do. Pastors caught in the demands of denominational and congregational pressures simply and courageously follow Christ. Decisions and directions in the marketplace are formed and framed by the singular influence of the Christ who values truth and integrity. Followers take their relational signals from Christ and embrace the worth of all people and elevate service to others as the highest of endeavors. Followers are liberated from the tyranny of the push-and-shove of outside influences that vie for control. The issue is settled: I'm a follower; it's just that simple.

A young homemaker related how she was liberated from the taunting demands for "significance" and found the peace and contentment that come to followers. She wrote,

> Thank you for the messages about "Followership."... they affirmed the lessons I've been learning.... He desires me to follow His steps, as I keep house for my husband and provide a contented environment for him.
>
> To do my household chores in a way pleasing to Christ... to keep attitudes and thoughts under His control, to be quiet, a keeper at home (Titus 2:4, 5)—in short, to be the best imitator of Christ that I can be in my home—where only Christ knows of my inner endeavors. To let the peace that comes from obedience suffice, where once others would encourage and praise my public efforts to DO for Christ, I'm learning to follow privately, and BE for Christ.
>
> So, thank you, for unknowingly reinforcing my newly discovered view of following.

A missionary, confronted with the conflicting expectations of his mission board, supporting churches, and fellow missionaries, confessed that he often felt drawn and quartered. Upon realizing anew that he was called to be a follower of Christ, he said, "I have never felt so liberated in all my life. I have sought to serve Christ by satisfying the expectations and demands of everyone but Christ. Now I just want to follow Him. I'll take my signals from Him."

A friend of mine broke down in tears as he told how his life had been whiplashed by his own desires and agendas. As he wept, he said, "I forgot about following Christ. I've gotten so scrambled up. It's so simple. I want to follow. I just want to follow Christ."

Starting out as a follower is the easy step.
Staying on the road with Him is the challenge.

Following Christ not only simplifies life, but also fills the follower with a riveting sense of wonder and awe. Christ is a most unusual and intriguing Person—not just in the supernatural manifestations of His divine power, but in the expressions of His day-to-day inter-actions with us. He will take us to places and unveil perspectives that we have never known. His compassion knows no stranger. His dis-dain for tradition and meaningless ritual is refreshing. Followers are awestruck by Christ's unlikely tolerance for, and interest in, scoundrels such as the sinners and tax collectors we read about in the Bible. Equally intriguing is His intolerance of religious hypocrisy and pride. His cleansing of the temple and His ministry of humble sensitivity show sides of His character that seem at once contradic-tory and compelling. His clarity of truth and arresting wisdom cap-ture the attention and imagination of followers. The fact that He came and could have taken any identity He wished, yet chose to cast Himself as a servant, creates an interest that draws us to want to know more of Him.

So it is with following. It's simply wonderful.

But—the simplicity and wonder of it all does not change the severe tension out of which following is born. The journey encoun-ters tremendous pressure that emerges from the depths of our own being. Starting out as a follower with a commitment to come after Him as the all-compelling center of life is the easy step. Staying on the road with Him is the challenge.

CHAPTER TWO

LIFE THE WAY IT WAS MEANT TO BE

Finding the Road Less Traveled

I was having lunch with a friend who is the head of management training at a major corporation. In the course of our conversation I mentioned a book I was reading about following as a strategic element in management and productivity. It was clear that he wasn't impressed as he brushed my remark aside and kept advancing his latest paradigms of top-down style and strategy. Bravely I brought up the subject again, and this time he all but laughed. I offered to send him a copy of the book if he would promise to read it. He said he would, but his enthusiasm was less than inspiring.

Let's face it, the concept of following as an all-consuming, non-negotiated, defining, and driving force of life has to struggle and scrape to find a place in a world that is bent on authority, status, power, and self-managed existence. Shelves in libraries and bookstores are jammed with books that deal with "self-help"—many written by people who get rich, ironically, by helping us help ourselves. The management section is packed with books on how to be a leader. I have seen only one on being a follower.

Seminars thrive on topics that relate to self-significance, self-sufficiency, and belief in ourselves as capable of managing and determining our destinies. I have yet to hear of a seminar on following.

Our mothers didn't help us either. I'd like to have a five dollar bill for every time I heard my mother say, "Joe, don't be a follower!" We lived in northern New Jersey, and she would usually add, "If all your friends jumped off the George Washington Bridge, would you?" What she didn't know was that I probably would: What would life be worth without your friends?

Journalist-historian Garry Wills captures the present cultural attitude toward followers when he writes:

> . . . followers are . . . a hazy and not very estimable lot—people to be dominated or served, mesmerized or flattered. We have thousands of books on leadership, none on followership. . . . The ideal seems to be a world in which everyone is a leader. . . . Talk about the nobility of leaders, the need for them, our reliance on them, raises the clear suspicion that followers are not so noble, not needed—that there is something demeaning about being a follower.[1]

The trouble with followership is that it is on a
collision course with a culture in which the prominent
goals are power, position, autonomy, and control.

The trouble with followership is that it is on a collision course with a culture in which the prominent goals are power, position, autonomy, and control. The thought of following raises huge questions about Christianity as a viable lifestyle. In the real world, someone who intentionally chooses to be a follower might be afraid of getting clobbered—or at least being taken advantage of, manipulated, marginalized, or trivialized. Few of us would readily choose such a vulnerable and subservient identity.

There is a reason why following suffers such bad press.

THE REASON IS WITHIN

Deep down, all of us cringe at the thought of giving up our independence to another's control. This resistance relates directly to our fallenness—the condition we inherited from birth.

Interestingly, God created us to follow. Being made in God's image means we are designed for a reflective following relationship to our Creator. Adam and Eve were given responsibilities that defined how they were to follow and then were released to enjoy all He had made. God was the singular pursuit of their lives, and their environment was a place to express their followership as an act of gratitude and love. And then followership, once a virtue, had its first bad day.

Life turned sour when these fully devoted followers were seduced by the offer of a supposedly better and more independent kind of life (Gen. 3:1–6). Adam and Eve took Satan's offer of a self-managed approach to life, and since then nothing we touch, taste, feel, or do has ever been the same—for any of us. Self-management is not only the essence of the first sin; it is the very character of sin itself.

Ironically, that primal pair gained anything but a better and more independent life. Everything broke around them. They became enslaved. They didn't cease to follow—it's just that they got locked into following their misguided, misdirected fallen instincts instead of God. Once proud, productive followers of their Creator, they now struggled as the pawns of an adversary who was bent on their destruction.

Actually, since we were designed to follow, we spend our entire lives following—it's just that no one wants to admit it. Sin strives for independence. The agony of sin is that the more we reach for autonomy, the more we become enslaved as followers. Strange, isn't it? The more we do life our way, the more we lose our independence. Whether the agent is drugs, food, work, sensual pleasure, alcohol, or self-centeredness, independent living leads its followers to disintegration.

Perhaps the greatest self-deceit is to tell
ourselves that we can be self-sufficient.

Perhaps the greatest self-deceit is to tell ourselves that we can be self-sufficient. That runs counter to our Creator's intention for us. We keep searching for something that can be found only in a restored relationship to Him, but the very thing we are searching for we refuse to find. The issue really is that we don't want to follow Christ.

Humanity is like a railroad car that has come unhooked from the engine, its source of power. As long as the car remains attached to the engine, with its intelligent, trained personnel on board, it is useful and productive. If it crosses a switch track and comes uncoupled, however, it seems to be detached and free of restriction— yet it is still forced to run a predetermined track. Only now the course lacks the safety and security of its connectedness to that which had given it meaning. It becomes motion without meaning.

THERE MUST BE SOMETHING MORE

Admiral Hyman Rickover served as a national leader for more than fifty years in one of the toughest enterprises, the U.S. Navy. By a special act of Congress, he was permitted to stay on active duty through his eighty-second year. A longtime associate recounted the last conversation he had with the admiral, who was then eighty-six and near death's door: "He acted as if he had been saving up the question: 'How are you supposed to know what God wants you to do with your life? Maybe I blew it. Maybe I should've been a cello player. What does life all add up to?'"

Al Kaline, the brilliant outfielder for the Detroit Tigers and a member of the Baseball Hall of Fame, was honored at a dinner attended by twenty-five hundred people. After he was introduced with a long litany of his achievements in baseball, he came to the podium to a standing ovation. During the course of his remarks he said, "There must be something more to life than this—chasing a lot of fly balls, getting a lot of base hits, making more money than you can spend."

When even the most avid self-managers admit they are still searching for meaning and fulfillment, it becomes evident that we were built to follow. Like overeaters always searching for the perfect diet, we restlessly probe for something to lead us to a more purposeful, meaningful existence. This sense of searching, from which we cannot escape, is present because we were created to live in a following relationship with a Superior Being who would show us the way. We are built to follow the One in whose image we were created. The purpose was to enable us to live connectedly with Someone who cared for us, who with superior wisdom and power could guide and protect us, Someone in whom we could find fulfillment and satisfaction. But sin uncoupled and diverted us. That explains the haunting sense inside us that there is Someone somewhere who could finally show us a more fulfilling, more meaningful way of life.

It is because we were meant to follow that independent living finally fails so dramatically.

Douglas Coupland, the author of several best-selling books about life at the end of this century, honestly discloses,

> Now—here is my secret:
>
> I tell it to you with an openness of heart that I doubt I shall ever achieve again, so I pray that you are in a quiet room as you hear these words. My secret is that I need God—that I am sick and can no longer make it alone. I need God to help me give, because I no longer seem to be capable of giving; to help me be kind, as I no longer seem capable of kindness; to help me love, as I seem beyond being able to love.[2]

Coupland speaks for millions in our day who have exhausted human hope and who hunger for a transcendent leader.

Julius Lester, professor of Judaistic studies at the University of Massachusetts at Amherst, writes of his students, "The need for transcendental meaning is as present in their lives as an open sore."[3]

Ted DeMoss, former chairman of the Christian Business Men's Committee, tells of a friend, John Herman, who had two earned Ph.D.s and whose lifelong ambition had been to meet the brilliant criminal lawyer Clarence Darrow, who had become famous in the Scopes "monkey trial." Late in Herman's life, it was arranged for the two men to meet. Sitting in the attorney's living room, Herman asked Darrow, "Now that you've come this far in life and you're not doing much lecturing or teaching or writing any more, how would you sum up your life?" Without hesitation, Darrow walked over to a coffee table and picked up a Bible. This took the guest by surprise, since Darrow was an atheist who had spent much of his life publicly ridiculing Scripture.

"This verse in the Bible describes my life." Darrow turned to the fifth chapter of Luke, the fifth verse. He changed the "we" to "I": "I have toiled all the night and have taken nothing."

He closed the Bible, put it back on the coffee table, and looked Herman straight in the face. "I have lived a life without purpose, without meaning, without direction. I don't know where I came from. And I don't know what I'm doing here. And worst of all, I don't know what's going to happen to me when I punch out of here."

Take it from those who have cut their own wake and arrived in the fantasyland of fame and fortune: We need something more in life than we can supply ourselves. Our hearts long for something beyond ourselves, for a cause that can give meaning and value to life and its assorted endeavors.

If independence were all it's cracked up to be, you would think that our lead-your-own-life culture would be overwhelmed by joy. Yet happiness increasingly eludes us.

No generation has been more free to live autonomously than ours. In our enlightened environment, anything and everything is okay as long as it satisfies and doesn't inflict damage on another. If independence were all it's cracked up to be, you would think that our lead-your-own-life culture would be overwhelmed by joy. Yet happiness increasingly eludes Americans. Singing "I Did It My Way" may have made Frank Sinatra a rich man, but doing things our way has never made us happy or fulfilled.

In a recent poll, Americans eighteen to twenty-four years of age responded that lack of family structure and guidance are their greatest concerns. Their inner quest for direction ranked higher than concern over AIDS, illiteracy, violence, or drugs.[4] It cannot go unnoticed that this generation, which has grown up in a thoroughgoing do-your-own-thing, anything-goes culture, has seen its suicide rate escalate by 300 percent.

LIFE'S ULTIMATE ADVENTURE

Amid this all too familiar emptiness and uncertainty, Jesus Christ invites us to accompany Him on an incredible journey toward a meaningful life, a secured future, and the power to significantly impact the world around us. From the rubble of life on our own terms, He rises like a phoenix and with boldness calls, "Follow Me."

When Christ entered the corridors of history, He made an incredible and compelling claim—a claim that no one else has been able to make with such confidence or affirmation in the lives of those who have embraced it. He said, "I am the way and the truth and the life" (John 14:6). Without shame or reservation, He claimed to be the defining and directing force of life. No other person in history has had so many convinced followers who were willing, not only to live for Him, but—after experiencing the reality of His claims and the pleasure of a relationship with Him—to die for Him as well.

Jesus Christ claims to be the reliable source to guide and direct our instincts toward both truth and life. No one yet, through all the centuries and in a variety of cultures, who has authentically followed Him without compromise has become disillusioned or found His ways to be disappointing.

Ironically, most of us who call ourselves Christians have not felt the need to become fully devoted followers of Christ. Like those outside the faith, we too search for meaning and happiness in this flat, plastic material world. We cling tenaciously to strategic points of independence. We soothe our conscience by following Him selectively when it seems convenient and self-gratifying. Then we wonder why Christianity seems sterile, ritualistic, burdensome, and sometimes boring. We, too, feel deep longings for meaning and purpose. We, likewise, feel twinges of loneliness at the core of our being—while the whole time we have in our own grasp the capacity to satisfy our souls and discover how life was meant to be. Like misers who go hungry because they refuse to buy food, we fear what

will happen if we pursue Christ without reservation as the uncompromised center of our existence.

No one yet who has authentically followed
Him without compromise has become disillusioned
or found His ways to be disappointing.

In the recent remake of the film *Sabrina*, Harrison Ford plays a
second-generation CEO who is savagely addicted to the growth and
gain of his inherited empire. When he meets the daughter of his family's chauffeur, she intrigues him and slowly but surely demonstrates
that there is more to life than the marketplace. As the lives of com-
moner and conqueror merge, he follows her to Paris. Drained and
ready for more to life, he says brokenly, "I've been following in footsteps all my life. Help me, Sabrina fair. You're the only one who can
save me."

This moving moment is a metaphor of our relationship to Christ
our Creator. We are tired and disillusioned, achieving success without significance. Addicted to what we thought were objects of liberation, and weary of working for an end that only leads to emptiness,
we look into the face of Christ, who has promised an abundant life.
In a wonderful moment of surrender, we say, "Help me. You are the
only One who can save me," and Christ replies, "Follow Me." It is
then that we begin life's ultimate adventure.

CHAPTER THREE

THE FOLLOWER IN ALL OF US

Submitting to the "Hound of Heaven"

Francis Thompson was consumed with life on his own terms. A poet of modest reputation, he lived and wrote in England during the reign of Queen Victoria. Although his father had urged him to study medicine, he left home to pursue the glitzy life of fame and fortune in London. He soon discovered, however, that he couldn't support himself in the world of literature and, disillusioned, soon became enslaved to opium and lived on the streets in pursuit of his drug habit.

A religious person in his upbringing, Thompson never lost complete sight of God. Yet he resisted Christ's call to follow, even amid his dissipated life.

A friend, Wilfred Meynell, rescued Thompson by promising to publish his poems. Reflecting on Christ's pursuit of him and his steadfast resistance, Thompson wrote his famous poem, "The Hound of Heaven." In it he reveals his deluded thought that in following Christ he would lose control and be left with a lesser life.

> *I fled Him, down the nights and down the days;*
> *I fled Him, down the arches of the years;*

I fled Him, down the labyrinthine ways
 Of my own mind; and in the mist of tears
I hid from Him, and under running laughter.
  Up vistaed hopes I sped;
  And shot, precipitated,
Adown Titanic glooms of chasmèd fears,
 From those strong Feet that followed, followed after.
  But with unhurrying chase,
  And unperturbèd pace,
 Deliberate speed, majestic instancy,
  They beat—and a Voice beat
  More instant than the Feet—
 'All things betray thee, who betrayest Me.' . . .
(For, though I knew His love Who followèd,
  Yet I was sore adread
Lest, having Him, I must have naught beside.)

Then, after describing his pilgrimage of fear and disillusionment, Thompson concludes with Christ's call:

'Rise, clasp My hand, and come'! . . .
Ah, fondest, blindest, weakest,
I am He Whom thou seekest![1]

There is something of Francis Thompson in us all. Even the best of us struggle with the notion that following Christ unconditionally will mean "doing without"—lacking what we could get out of life on our own. We wonder what becoming a fully devoted follower might cost us. It could require an integrity that would inhibit career advancement. Could it mean the loss of a friendship, the altering of a dream, a life without sensation and pleasure? Our doubts arise from the old notion that if we fully follow, He will send us to some faraway land infested with bugs and snakes and animistic rituals—or, at least, that life will be a somber spiritual chore without the bells and whistles we have come to enjoy. That "lest having Him I must have naught beside" feeling still haunts and hinders us.

Yet persistently, insistently, Christ pursues us and welcomes us back to life the way it was meant to be. It is life in a delightful but dependent following relationship with a transcendent power and a wise guide who leads us toward His glory and our good. The advantage is ours. We who have been redeemed have been found by Him. He has reached out to clasp our hands in His. He has made us His own. For us, the search for life at its fullest is only a commitment away.

We wonder what becoming a
fully devoted follower might cost us.

But though we are happy to belong to Him, we still resist the thought of unconditionally following Him. Our passion for independence is stubborn, and we choose to ignore the yearnings we recognize in the core of our souls.

We should not be surprised that Christ's call to a following relationship with Him goes against the grain. Our fallenness is full of the seductive influence of that bogus offer of a better life apart from God. Not only were we born with this notion implanted in our sinful nature, but we live in a world managed and controlled by the very one who still hawks the destructive offer on the streets of our culture. Because Satan is the god of our age, we find ourselves in the midst of an upside-down, inside-out world that seeks to connect with the wrongness of its fallen nature. The truth is, we live in an upside-down world. This explains why Christ's teaching so often flew in the face of the general climate of His society. To a world convinced that gain was measured in the accumulation of things, He said, "What good will it be for a man if he gains the whole world, yet forfeits his soul?" (Matt. 16:26). Christ taught that the way to gain something is to give it away. The key to living is dying to self. Greatness is achieved through serving. Independence is not to be valued, but rather the submission of the follower, who then ultimately becomes useable, effective, and fulfilled.

After reading the book I sent him, my consultant friend responded with repentant enthusiasm. The concept of the preeminent value of following had unlocked for him new paradigms of effective and productive results in the marketplace. He said it would be required reading for all his trainees. In principle the book didn't offer a new idea, but an ancient truth that we have buried under our illicit love affair with leadership and control.

> *Leaders cast a vision and set strategy, but it*
> *is the followers, the foot soldiers, who guarantee*
> *the outcomes and bring the vision to fruition.*

That following is what we were originally designed for is almost self-evident in the fact that everyone can follow but very few have either the talent or the opportunity to lead. Consider that the impact of almost any endeavor is actualized through followers. Leaders cast a vision and set strategy, but it is the followers, the foot soldiers, who guarantee the outcomes and bring the vision to fruition. It is not a coincidence that Scripture goes to great pains to instruct followers.

FOLLOWING COMES FIRST

Even those who lead must first of all be followers. In the marketplace, it is the capacity to be devoted followers of company policy and sacrificial contributors to the vision and dictates of someone above and beyond that qualifies a potential leader for advancement. Even when a person becomes a leader, there is submission to a board of directors, stockholders, generally accepted management practices, and the requirements of the national corporate environment. Much of a CEO's success relates to how well he follows these larger realities that loom above, around, and beyond him.

Spiritual leaders are only effective when they lead as non-negotiated followers. Think of the leaders you know who have in some way failed. Whether it was a moral, financial, or relational failure, or something else, it inevitably occurred because at some point the person ceased to be a follower of Christ. The evangelist Jimmy Swaggart, who confessed to consorting with a prostitute, admitted that he had become so successful that he thought that he was above the law. That was an implicit admission that he had ceased to be a follower and had determined that he could be the master of his destiny.

Rarely is a leadership disaster rooted in the person's incapacity to lead. It is most often an issue of failed followership. In fact, all of our failures can ultimately be traced to ceasing to follow Christ. Yet our twisted sense of values, exalting leading over following, independence over dependence, is evident in our whole attitude toward those whom we regard as qualified to lead and the qualifications we consider essential for the task. We are too easily seduced by the external qualities of charisma, competence, and credentials. This is not to say that these elements aren't important. It is to underscore that these are not the primary qualifiers. But American society refuses to accept the idea that character and submission to moral authority are important, particularly in the selection of leaders.

> *Rarely is a leadership disaster rooted*
> *in the person's incapacity to lead. It is most*
> *often an issue of failed followership.*

We would rather choose leaders that enable us to prosper peacefully. If they can do that, then character is a mute point. In an interview in *Time* magazine, Karen Harris-Heidenreich, speaking of the importance of continued government health care, said, "Look, if Clinton can change this country, then he can have all the affairs that he wants and he can even run his own savings and loan."[2]

Her opinion would find resounding support.

When God chooses leaders, He chooses those who have a heart to follow Him. Unfortunately, even some of God's best people have made the mistake of assuming that external qualifications for leadership were God's criteria also. Consider Samuel, the great prophet of Israel, who was on assignment to choose a king to replace Saul. Saul had the altitude—Scripture notes that he was an impressive man who stood head and shoulders above everyone else (1 Sam. 9:2)—but he was seriously deficient in attitude and eventually disqualified himself by doing the king thing his own way.

So Samuel went to Bethlehem to the house of Jesse. As he surveyed Jesse's sons, he was struck with the external qualities of Eliab, and thought, "'Surely the LORD's anointed stands here before the LORD.' But the LORD said to Samuel, 'Do not consider his appearance or his height, for I have rejected him. The LORD does not look at the things man looks at. Man looks at the outward appearance, but the LORD looks at the heart'" (1 Sam. 16:6–7).

God's choice was the youngest son, who was so unlikely a prospect that he was left in the field to tend the family herd. But this boy would be known for the rest of his life as a leader who was first and foremost a follower. He became known as "a man after [God's] own heart" (1 Sam. 13:14). The only blemish on his record appeared in a moment when he ceased to be a follower of God and chased after his own instincts instead.

Reflecting the character of Christ as a follower gives a leader a platform of respect that draws people to him. Following Christ instead of our own whims develops a strength that is admired and creates a model for others to follow. There is no doubt about it: A leader—a good and effective leader—is, at the core, consumed with following.

Leaders, if they will be persons of lasting and effective impact, never view themselves as anything but followers.

Billy Graham has been a consistent model of the fully devoted follower throughout his long ministry as a world-renowned evangelist. Nowhere is that more evident than in regard to his character. If anyone could have been seduced by the pride of popularity, the lure of potential wealth, a passion for power and control, it would have been he. Yet, through all the years of blazing headlines, friendships with presidents, international recognition, and huge evangelistic success, Billy Graham has remained an undaunted follower of Christ. His humility, selfless passion for the cause of Christ, and unassuming posture in the light of great and unusual gifts have marked him with a Christlikeness that has been the continuing reason for the respect and credibility that the gospel has been granted through him. With Billy it was always Christ at the center. As big as Billy's profile was, it was never big enough to eclipse the Christ around whom all of his life revolved.

Leaders, if they will be persons of lasting and effective impact, never view themselves as anything but followers. This is why Paul said to the Corinthians, "Follow my example, as I follow the example of Christ" (1 Cor. 11:1).

WHY DON'T WE GET IT?

As clear as Scripture is about the priority and preeminence of following, it is somewhat amazing that we still don't seem to get it. Churches hold leadership training courses, but rarely get around to talking about following. We fill our preaching agendas with calls for men to be leaders in their homes and leaders in the church, when what we really need are people who are first and foremost fully devoted followers.

Mothers, husbands, fathers, pastors, and bosses are at their best when their commitment to following Christ is uncompromised and evident. Think of the dramatic power of a husband who tenderly cares for his wife, because he is singularly defined and directed by Christ, regardless of what he gets in return or of how she is responding. As a follower he has no option but to live Christ's love in his home. Or consider a leader whose singular goal is to magnify Christ and serve the needs of His people rather than gaining a reputation and influence.

Yet our books, church programs, small-group studies, workshops, and seminars are spun more toward self-help, personal worth, significance, and leadership than on the characteristics of the follower, such as trust, devotion, and dependence.

I regularly receive letters and calls from pulpit committees looking for pastoral replacements. Usually their queries deal with issues of credentials and leadership competence; matters such as age, experience, the size of previous congregations, preaching and leading abilities, and the length of stay at previous pastorates dominate the conversation. If we really knew what was important, talk about followership would occupy far more time in our selection of leaders.

I work in educational marketing and have to admit that, like many other schools, we have said, in essence, "Send us your students and we will make leaders of them." This is particularly troubling, since long before any of us can be successful leaders in any endeavor—especially spiritual endeavors—we must first prove ourselves as committed followers. And what of the vast majority of students and others who are not built to be leaders, never will be leaders, and would not only fail as leaders but be terribly frustrated if they tried to be? We should be saying, "Send us students and we will make followers of them."

Leading is a temporary assignment;
following is a lifelong calling.

Scripture underscores that leadership is an attribute that should not be plotted and planned for, but something developed through the character of followership (1 Tim. 3). Even then, being granted position and power is the prerogative of a sovereign God who will act in His time and in His way. God moves through the masses of His people to select a few to lead, not because they are superior people but because as followers they have become qualified for leadership. This is why leaders who have emerged because of their own schemes and their desires for personal gain run great risks. They get to be leaders by self-promotion and manipulation. When they mount the platform and are empowered, they will still be driven by self-advancing notions and use both God's work and other people for self-enhancement.

Following is the mark of the most successful leaders. Yet, when our task of leading is done, we ourselves will still be followers. Leading is a temporary assignment; following is a lifelong calling.

OUR WAY OR THE HIGH WAY?

The fact that most of us don't aspire to power and influence in the public square does not mean that the leadership impulse is absent from our souls. It is alive and well in all of us in our desire to control our own destinies. Uninterested in positions of leadership, we are still bent on maintaining personal control over our own lives, and that is our fatal flaw.

The call of Christ to follow means rejecting impulses of control, independence, and self-actualization. It requires us to submit both our wills and our wants to Him and His better way. All of us will spend our whole life following; the issue is who or what we follow. Christ welcomes us to the road less traveled, but the road that is by far the better way.

E. Stanley Jones, a missionary to India in the first half of this century, wrote of following Christ,

> Some are in self—they are determined by self-interest primarily—it is the driving force of their lives. To get and to get on for self is the compelling motive. Some are "in the herd." Before they act, they look around—they don't act; they only react to what the herd does. The roots of their motives are in "What will people think?" Making self, or the herd, our god, is sin, the chief sin.
>
> To be "in Christ" means to pull up the roots of one's very life from the soil of sin and self and herd and plant them "in Christ." He becomes the source of our life, the source of our thinking, our feeling, our acting, our being.
>
> This obviously involves self-surrender. Not merely the surrender of our sins, our bad habits, our wrong thinking and our wrong motives, but of the very self behind all these. All of these are symptoms; the unsurrendered self is the disease. So the phrase "in Christ" is not only the ultimate concept, but it demands the ultimate act, self-surrender. The only thing we own is just ourselves. We don't own our money, our property, not even the house we live in, for we will leave it all behind. The only thing we will take out with us is just ourselves. It is the only thing we own. That one thing we own—the self—is deliberately handed back to the Giver in an act of supreme self-surrender with words something like these: "I can't handle this self of mine. Take me as I am, and make me as I ought to be. I give myself and my sins and my problems to Thee; but myself first and foremost. I've been 'in myself'; now I am 'in Thee.'" We lose ourselves, and to our astonishment, find ourselves. We live when we live "in Him."[3]

By far our greatest challenge is the transfer of personal authority from ourselves to Him. Even though we call Him Christ and refer to Him as Lord, few of us want Him to be the leader unconditionally. We live with the sense that we can do a pretty good job of managing our own lives. We will listen to His advice and keep Him on hand in case of an emergency, but to transfer full authority to Him is less than appealing. Besides, how do we know that Christ won't take us somewhere we don't want to go or require something we don't want to give? So we choose to be just "normal" Christians. We will even give and serve. But our destinies will be crafted on the drawing board of our own wants and way.

Until we know the danger and folly of notions like these, we will remain vulnerable to the sorrow and consequence of the wrong-way thrust of our self-directed instincts.

Lewis Carroll's classic work *Alice's Adventures in Wonderland* speaks volumes when Alice asks the Cheshire Cat for directions:

> "Would you tell me, please, which way I ought to go from here?"
> "That depends a good deal on where you want to get to," said the Cat.
> "I don't much care where—" said Alice.
> "Then, it doesn't matter which way you go," said the Cat.[4]

Unfortunately for Alice, for Francis Thompson, and for us, it makes a huge difference which way we go and whom we follow. Fortunately, the Hound of Heaven still pursues us, urging, "Rise, clasp My hand and come! . . . Ah, fondest, blindest, weakest, I am He whom thou seekest!"

CHAPTER FOUR

THE TYRANNY OF SELF-DIRECTED LIVING

Why We Need a Leader

Roy Riegels was a walk-on football player for the University of California. At six-feet-even he was about average for players of his era. He was the center for the freshman team, and as a sophomore he was a starter on the varsity team ahead of seasoned players like Andy Miller and "Fat Glasgow." He distinguished himself by missing only nine minutes of playing time for the next three years. Benny Lom, the heralded tailback on the team, says that "Roy was one of Cal's great centers. . . . In three years he never centered a bad snap. He was a smart player with a good sense of timing." But few remember that.

It is not his competence that is remembered; it's his moment of disorientation that has marked the rest of his life.

Cal was facing Georgia Tech in the Rose Bowl that January in 1929, and as the team walked off the bus, Riegels could hardly believe that in his sophomore year he would be playing in the Rose Bowl.

Little did he know.

It was a scoreless game when Georgia Tech's Thompson took a handoff around the end for a fifteen-yard gain. Cal's Irv Phillips hit him and knocked the ball loose. Riegels, who as a center never got to run with the ball, grabbed the ball as it bounced into his arms. He eluded two players, saw clear running space, and with every muscle straining at the prospect of unexpected glory, he raced toward the goal line sixty-five yards away.

The wrong goal line—his own end zone.

Thinking that his teammates, yelling from the sidelines, were cheering him on toward his moment of destiny, he was dumfounded when Lom, who had been running after him, caught him at the one yard line and turned him around, only to be immediately buried under a swarm of Tech players. On the next play, the Cal quarterback was taken down behind the goal line for a two-point safety for Georgia Tech. California lost the game by one point.

Riegels later recalled that as he was running, he heard Lom in pursuit yelling, "Stop! You're going the wrong way!" Roy thought, *What's wrong with him!* He would soon find out and never forget what was wrong since he was known from that time on as "Wrong Way Riegels." One commentator has noted that he is "a legend among bumblers." Everywhere he went and whenever he was introduced, that moment stuck to his person like a tattoo. In fact, when Jim Marshall, playing for the Minnesota Vikings, ran a San Francisco fumble a full sixty yards into his own end zone in 1964, the announcer screamed into the microphone in disbelief, "Jim Marshall has pulled a Wrong Way Riegels here today!" Riegels' misdirected run remains one of the most memorable incidents in the history of football. It is without a doubt the most replayed sports moment on national television.

To what does Roy Riegels owe this honor? Instincts without direction. As well intended as he was, even his sincerity could not shield him from a misdirected moment.

In that life-changing chase for glory, Riegels simply followed his instincts. They weren't bad instincts—just instincts without an orientation that could guide him to success instead of shame. Everything within him had a clear sense that what he was doing was right. He was convinced that he was on the verge of national acclaim. Granted, in the course of the weightier issues of life, running the wrong way was a rather innocent miscue, but the reality is that his disorientation had betrayed him. What he thought was right was in the end a source of lifelong regret.

LIFE BY RAW INSTINCT

Wrong Way Riegels' legacy is a metaphor of our own lives. Our instincts to run with the ball of life are often well intended but disconnected from an orientation to the ways of Christ. Our Christianity is dismembered, not always by radical rebellion, but more often by careless disregard. And unfortunately, we sometimes remain completely unaware that life is going the wrong way until we are buried under a pile of disappointing results.

We sometimes remain completely unaware
that life is going the wrong way until we are
buried under a pile of disappointing results.

It just seems right, doesn't it, to seek to satisfy some of our material wants? After all, look how much other people have, and think of how happy we could be if we, too, could share in the spoils of this affluent culture without much thought to the principles that would both direct and restrict us. The availability of credit and quick cash often find us accumulating large amounts of debt, and the things we thought would bring happiness instead create a burden that haunts us with fear and uncertainty. Worse yet, we often try to dig ourselves out of our dilemma by chasing get-rich-quick schemes, taking additional employment, or postponing the day of judgment on one credit card by taking out another. Our sense of security and the stability of significant relationships collapse under the weight of debt. We didn't really intend for life to turn out this way. We just lived by our instincts.

Didn't we hear the pursuing Christ chasing us, saying, "Be content with what you have" ... "Seek first his kingdom and his righteousness, and all these things will be given to you as well" ... "Store up for yourselves treasures in heaven" (Heb. 13:5; Matt. 6:33, 20).

Even such mundane things as food instinctively consumed can produce a backlash. Who doesn't struggle with a love of eating? I have a love-hate relationship with my bathroom scale—mostly hate. I don't wake up in the morning planning to chub up. It's just that I graze throughout the day, out of habit and instinct. Then comes the mad search for diets, with their tyrannical and torturous routines. A friend asked me whether I had ever considered the garlic diet. I asked how much weight could be lost on a diet like that. The reply was, "Not much. But people just stay farther away, and you look smaller from a distance."

It's hard to tell what I might look like if it weren't for the interest of my wife, Martie, in what the scale says when I get on it. The issue for me is not so much the weight as it is that husbands who are fully devoted followers love their wives with the sensitivity and sacrifice with which Christ loves the church (Eph. 5:25ff.). If my weight is important to my wife, then following Christ means it's important to me.

Think of the words that we have instinctively spoken even to people we love but have come to regret later on. It's not that we planned to be verbally brutal; it just seemed to be the right thing to say at that moment. It's what we wanted to say, what we needed to say to protect ourselves and control the event. Yet after all is said, memories linger and scars develop from which we may never recover.

Didn't we hear Christ trying to intercept us as He called us to words that help and heal?

THE DARKER SIDE

There is a darker side to our instinctive behavior. We put ourselves in particular peril when, regardless of the consequences, we permit our instincts to drive us to do what we already know is wrong.

Samantha was young, vivacious, and single. She had grown up in a solid home where the ways of Christ had been honored. Active in the ministries of her church, she always wanted to reflect well on Christ in the office where she worked. She knew that Richard had a troubled marriage, and she felt that she needed to be sensitive to him and his problems. In fact, she had even prayed that she could be used to turn his heart toward Christ as the solution to his dilemma.

They began to spend time together on breaks. Richard felt cared-for as he poured out his heart to her listening ear. Then they went out for a sandwich at lunch time, then stopped at the local deli after work. Soon Samantha realized that the intrigue had changed the agenda of her heart. She felt the alluring sense of danger mingled with the sense of adventure and self-fulfillment. She was at a crossroads. Would it be Christ or Richard?

She chose Richard.

We put ourselves in particular peril when, regardless of the consequences, we permit our instincts to drive us to do what we already know is wrong.

I still remember being warned by my father not to touch the glowing end of the cigarette lighter in our car. It was a new car, and cigarette lighters at that time were a newfangled accessory. Since our family didn't smoke, cigarette paraphernalia were not only foreign to this young boy, but intriguing as well. It was a Saturday morning, and since no one was outside, I opened the door to the car, slid across the front seat, and punched in the cigarette lighter to see what would happen. When the lighter popped back, I pulled it out and was taken by the warmth and orange glow of the coil. I remember taking a hair and watching it shrivel and curl as the smoke rose. Then I took my thumb and touched it to the coils. I can recall the smell that emitted from the contact of my flesh to the lighter—it felt like a branding iron. As I yanked my thumb away, I could see the circular imprint of the coils burned into my thumb.

The number is legion who have been burned or branded by allowing their instincts to drive them over the boundaries. The damage from instinctive immorality, greed, self-centeredness, abuse, brutality, manipulation, and control is massive.

What happened to the sailors on the *U.S.S. Indianapolis* toward the close of World War II is a pointed illustration of the seductive pressures in life that tempt us to abandon restraint.

Ed Harrell, who was to serve as a trustee at Moody later on, was a Marine on assignment to guard a high-security shipment put on board the heavy cruiser in California in July 1945. The shipment was so highly classified that even the captain of the *Indianapolis* didn't know what it was. It was to be dropped at a mid-Pacific island. Only after the war ended did Harrell and the rest of the crew learn that the secret cargo was components for the atomic bomb that would be dropped on Hiroshima. With the mission accomplished, the cruiser set sail for the Philippines. En route, it crossed paths with a Japanese submarine that drilled its hull with torpedoes. The *Indianapolis* sank quickly, forcing Ed Harrell and at least 700 other sailors to abandon ship in life jackets in the salty waters more than a thousand miles from their destination. Only 316 of the 1,196 persons from the *Indianapolis* survived.

In their training, naval officers had been instructed that if their ship were to be sunk, two things were vital for survival of the crew. Number one, they were to try to stay together in large groups in the ocean. Number two, they were to never drink the salt water.

Because the mission was top secret, no one knew the location of the *U.S.S. Indianapolis*, and no one missed it when it went down. For days, these sailors bobbed in the Pacific under the scorching sun. Ed Harrell recalls seeing the fins of sharks swimming nearby. Periodically some sailors would leave the groups to launch out on their own, hoping to find land. And these sailors, who had followed their misguided instincts, were taken by the sharks.

For days, Harrell and the rest went undiscovered. The sun baked and dehydrated them. The agony of thirst was almost unbearable. Several sailors, in desperation, gulped salt water, and as a result they became deranged and ultimately violent. Ed remembers seeing them hallucinating that their comrades had drinking water, and he even saw one sailor stab another to death in order to possess what he thought was a fresh-water canteen.

> *"O foolish creatures that destroy*
> *Themselves for transitory joy."*

When the urges became the strongest, that was the moment when the discipline of restraint became strategically important.

One of Aesop's fables drives home the point of the treachery of indulgent passions:

> *A jar of honey chanced to spill*
> *Its contents on the windowsill*
> *In many a viscous pool and rill.*
>
> *The flies, attracted by the sweet,*
> *Began so greedily to eat,*
> *They smeared their fragile wings and feet.*
>
> *With many a twitch and pull in vain*
> *They gasped to get away again,*
> *And died in aromatic pain.*
>   *Moral*
> *O foolish creatures that destroy*
> *Themselves for transitory joy.[1]*

You can't help but think of the warning, "There is a way that seems right to a man, but in the end it leads to death" (Prov. 14:12).

APPLAUSE FOR ABANDONING RESTRAINT

To make matters worse, living by raw, unrestrained instincts is endorsed by a society that encourages us to embrace the notion that life is a random series of glory runs managed by our own sense of direction. Our generation places a high priority on cutting our own wake in life.

And it's not just because we are proud, intentional pagans. This generation in America has experienced disappointment, betrayal, and abandonment from the institutions and authorities that have guided and directed them in the past. For many, home, government, education, church, and other basic institutions have become not only disappointing but unreliable. All we have left is ourselves and our own instincts.

To make matters worse, society long ago scrapped any thought of the validity of managing life according to an external authority. Autonomy, self-determination, and self-actualization are now held to be inalienable rights. In fact, the general consensus today is that if you try to impose any kind of moral authority, you are suspected of manipulation and control. This affirmation of moral independence as a primary value affects our attitude toward every relationship and activity of life.

David Wells, a theologian and a keen observer of American culture, notes,

> Amidst all of the abundance and the technological marvels of our time, what is true and what is right have lost their hold upon our society. They have lost their saliency, their capacity to shape life. Today, our moral center is gone. It is not merely that secularization has marginalized God, relegating him to the outer edges of our public life from whence he becomes entirely irrelevant, but we have also lost our understanding of ourselves as moral beings. In our private universe, as in that which is public, there is no center.[2]

Few things clearly symbolize American society's disdain for transcendent moral authority as well as MTV's popular Bevis and Butthead cartoon sitcom. In sequence after sequence, this pair trashes anything that represents guidance or restraint. Education, family, church, civic authority, teachers, and other institutions or individuals who represent traditional norms and values are mocked and held in disrespect. Bevis and his sidekick lead lives that are unashamedly self-consumed and self-directed, and it is clear that nothing is out of bounds for them as long as they can get away with it. They are particularly blatant in their trashing of Christian values. In one episode they wander into a youth meeting of the Christian Business Men's Committee. Upon spotting them on the stage, the crowd angrily shouts taunts at them. They flee for their safety, leaving the clear impression that groups that represent religious authority are particularly hateful and hostile toward the youth of this generation.

In a sense, ours is a Bevis and Butthead world where external moral governance is to be ignored, scorned, or violated, sometimes just for the sake of flaunting our own independence. We live in a world where Madonna, without censure or critique, can publicly pronounce that life by her raw sexual instincts is a spiritual experience.

Advertisers spend millions to understand where people are and then to appeal to them on their turf. Moral restraint is obviously out of favor when Nike sells shoes with a slogan like "Just Do It" and Burger King trumpets, "Sometimes you gotta break the rules." Bacardi Black Rum markets the notion, "Some people embrace the night because rules of the day do not apply." Easy Spirit shoes "conform to your foot so you don't have to conform to anything." And even Merrill Lynch declares, "Your world should know no boundaries."

When professional basketball player Dennis Rodman was traded to Chicago, more Rodman Bulls jerseys were sold more quickly than when Michael Jordan announced his return to the Bulls from baseball. You have to live in Chicago to know what a significant statistic that is—especially given the fact that Rodman's lifestyle so radically counteracts moral restraint. His tattooed body, which is pierced for decorative accessories in his nose, navel, and nipples, has been dressed in drag and used in various aberrant activities that he publicly acknowledges.

"Just Do It" sells more than shoes.
The slogan has become life's managing ethic.

"Just Do It" sells more than shoes. The slogan has become life's managing ethic. The only problem is that just doing it didn't work for Wrong Way Riegels, and it won't ultimately work for us. Just doing it when it best serves our interests and instincts will in the end leave us betrayed and broken.

DISAPPOINTING RESULTS

Jurist Robert Bork observes that the decline in American culture driven by its own independence is "widespread, ranging across virtually the entire society, from the violent underclass of the inner cities to our cultural and political elites, from rap music to literary studies, from pornography to law, from journalism to scholarship, from union halls to universities. Wherever one looks, the traditional virtues of this culture are being lost, its vices multiplied, its values degraded—in short, the culture itself is unraveling." He adds that one of the underlying reasons for the skyrocketing crime rates, the devastation both personally and culturally from drugs, the rise of illegitimacy, the decline of civility, and the increasing vulgarity of popular entertainment is that we have taken the concept of "liberty" and turned it into "radical individualism"—which he defines as "a refusal to admit limits to the gratification of the self." He notes that the elements driving our culture refuse "to make distinctions about morality or aesthetics based on any transcendent principle. There is no such principle, only sensation, energy, the pleasure of the moment, and the expansion of self." And given our addiction to the instinct of pleasure, he concludes, we live in a culture that has come to believe that pleasure can "be maximized only by freedom from authority."[3]

The ancient prophet Isaiah spoke to the decadence of his day in terms that sound all too familiar today.

> *Woe to those who call evil good and good evil,*
> *who put darkness for light and light for darkness . . .*
> *Woe to those who are wise in their own eyes*
> *and clever in their own sight.*

He then spoke of the certain outcomes of their arrogant, self-managed lifestyle.

> *Therefore, as tongues of fire lick up straw*
> *and as dry grass sinks down in the flames,*
> *so their roots will decay*
> *and their flowers blow away like dust;*
> *for they have rejected the law of the LORD Almighty*
> *and spurned the word of the Holy One of Israel.*

(Isa. 5:20–21, 24)

We live in the midst of a strange paradox in America. Over the last two decades we have been aggressively restricting physical freedom for the sake of public safety. From seat belts to helmets, from stringent health codes to condoms, we have been willing to inconvenience ourselves and go to great expense to protect our lives and environment from the damage that occurs when we are unregulated. But at the same time, we disdain any thought of the kind of moral restraint that guarantees peace and fulfillment in the aspects of life that truly count.

"The freedom of our day," declared a Harvard valedictorian, "is the freedom to devote ourselves to any values we please, on the mere condition that we do not believe them to be true."[4]

FOLLOWING RECONSIDERED

The obvious failure of managing life by unrestrained instincts should at least make us attentive when someone wiser and greater comes alongside and says, "Follow Me."

When Christ recruited His disciples, He was up-front about the issue. He did not deceive and dupe them into following. "Follow Me" was the first thing and the last thing Christ said to Peter. It is for us, as well, the beginning and the end of everything. All of life in between is measured by the call.

> *"Follow Me" was the first thing and the last*
> *thing Christ said to Peter. It is for us, as well,*
> *the beginning and the end of everything.*

Effective living begins with a choice to follow and continues as an uncompromised and non-negotiated commitment to becoming fully devoted to Christ. God knew that our instincts needed a scheme in which they could be managed toward success. Even before sin raised its problematic challenge to life, God instituted a basic set of directives and warnings to shield that first couple in Eden from the treachery of urges without guidance. It is instructive for us to remember that life didn't go south on them until they chose not to submit their instincts to God's clear directions. At that point everything about them and their environment radically changed; in the process they exchanged satisfaction for shame, delight for disappointment.

The challenge to us who want to be fully devoted followers is that our commitment must express itself with increasing measures of consistency in a world that trumpets the importance of charting our own course. Nor is it just the world out there that challenges our commitment. Those internal promptings of our own fallenness gang up with the present cultural climate to distract and seduce us. When we give in to the allure of society's sense of freedom, our instincts take over. Whether it be the instinct of greed, power, position, testosterone, peace, significance, security, prosperity, or protection, we become self-led and are encouraged not to yield an inch of ground to the authority of anyone who threatens our grip on life. Then we discover in the end that we have run the wrong way.

Jeffrey Dahmer, who brutalized, butchered, and cannibalized countless young men in homosexual passion, said in a moment of sane reflection, "I should have never left God."

It was far too late.

It is a scary commentary on life that, left to ourselves, we self-destruct.

Seeking, selecting, and trusting a leader is life's most strategic pursuit. We who have embraced Christ as redeemer and friend need to do more than call Him Lord. We must embrace Him as the unqualified leader of our lives. He is the only leader we can trust.

CHAPTER FIVE

THE COMPELLING CHRIST

Why Wouldn't You Follow?

When we think of names like Hitler, Mussolini, the Ayatollah Khomeini, Mu'ammar Khaddafi, Saddam Hussein, and most recently Shoko Asahara—accused of a poison gas attack in a Tokyo subway— it is not their ruthless behavior that made them dominant as much as the fact that millions of people followed them. These leaders were, or are, trusted by the masses. They were leaders in whom sincere people placed their hopes for liberation, meaning, fulfillment, and a better life, only to find themselves disappointed and damaged.

So we are not the first to set out in pursuit of finding and following a compelling leader. Many throughout history, upon realizing that a self-led life driven by instincts is insufficient, have searched for someone or something to follow. These seekers have been drawn to social revolutionaries, philosophers, politicians, and—unfortunately— assorted groups of charlatans who promise wealth and fulfillment in exchange for just a little cash. The very fact that there have always been throngs looking for someone to give life a sense of safety, order, and a cause worth living for is a clear commentary on our intrinsic need for finding meaning and direction outside ourselves.

Chuck Colson speaks of this in his book *Kingdoms in Conflict* as he recalls his days in the White House as special counsel to former President Nixon.

> One brisk December night as I accompanied the president from the Oval Office in the West Wing of the White House to the Residence, Mr. Nixon was musing about what people wanted in their leaders. He slowed a moment, looking into the distance across the South Lawn, and said, "The people really want a leader a little bigger than themselves, don't they, Chuck?" I agreed. "I mean someone like de Gaulle," he continued. "There's a certain aloofness, a power that's exuded by great men that people feel and want to follow."[1]

This generation is not quite as ready, as Nixon assumed, to turn one's life and destiny over to another who will shape and form it at their will.

Ray Carter works in the upscale section of Chicago known as Lincoln Park. It is full of what sociologists call "Busters" and "Squires," most of them single. Busters are the emerging generation on the American landscape and are so-called because everything in their world is broken. Squires are Busters who are more established, with better jobs and a relatively stable prospect for the future. But Squires share the perspectives and attitudes of Busters. Ray tells me that since every major institution and organization that surrounds Busters' lives has either disappointed or betrayed them, they find it almost impossible to trust anyone but themselves and those who are exactly like themselves. For them—as quite frankly it is for most of us—reticence to turn everything over to a leader, even to Christ, results not so much from stubbornness as from a feeling of distrust.

The fear of following does not always arise
from rebellion; more often, it's a matter of trust.

Ray put his finger on much of the problem in a note he wrote to me recently.

The issue with Busters is not so much rebellion against authority or institutions as it is suspicion and fear of trusting authority figures that have betrayed them and institutions that have used them. This next generation has grown up in a world of fractured relationships and an American Dream they believe will never be theirs. In a world such as this, who does one have but themselves and others like themselves? This mind-set is seen in the words of the theme song to the sitcom "Friends."

Then Ray quoted the words to that song: "So no one told you life was going to be this way . . . I'll be there for you ('cause you're there for me too)."

We don't have to be Busters to identify with their fear of following. Their feeling does not always arise from rebellion; more often, it's a matter of trust.

How do you unconditionally trust an authority figure when your deepest scars are memories of being abused by your parent? How do you cultivate a trusting, dependent relationship when you come from a broken home? How do you cultivate a concern for the direction your life is going when you don't believe there is a future worth caring about? A Buster quoted the following, a poem by Langston Hughes, on the Internet—a sign that the feelings of despair given voice earlier in this century are still prevalent today:

What happens to a dream deferred?
Does it dry up
Like a raisin in the sun?
Or fester like a sore—
And then run?
Does it stink like rotten meat?
Or crust and sugar over—
Like a syrupy sweet?

Maybe it just sags
Like a heavy load.

Or does it explode?[22]

The reality this generation has inherited is that someone has shrunk their world to the significance of the immediate. And since there is really nothing currently to hope in or to trust, the question of what to do with the rest of life is irrelevant. There is a troubling paradox for those who are born into this generation. What they want the most—meaningful relationships—they are afraid of the most. Wanting guidance and direction, they feel that there is no one they can trust.

As I walked home from work one day, a young woman was walking toward me and wearing an unusual sweatshirt. It depicted a face with the chin resting on the figure's hand and under the rather expressionless look was the word "Whatever." That word seems to embody the feelings of this generation. Happily, life is more than "whatever" when it is released to the dynamic direction that Christ can give. But without Christ as leader, "whatever" is the honest appraisal of life.

It is not just this generation that has trouble trusting. How many of us have been betrayed by relationships into which we put our trust, or hurt by people whom we have been willing to follow? Politics, education, and even the church at large have all fostered a sense of cynicism that has left us with little to trust in except ourselves and those who think and live the way we do.

> *"Whatever." That word seems to embody*
> *the feelings of the Buster generation.*

No doubt most of us like the sound of trusting Christ as leader of our lives. We know we need a leader and believe He could be the one. But we are stuck in places where we can't see Him clearly enough; along the way, someone stepped between us and blocked Christ from view. That someone may have been a parent who neglected or abused us yet was regarded by everyone else as a respectable Christian. That someone may have been a trusted spiritual leader who took advantage of us, or a Christian colleague who cheated or mistreated us, or a friend who claims to be a follower but bitterly refuses to forgive another. These failed trust relationships are like an eclipse of the sun. When the moon, which ordinarily reflects the light of the sun, gets in the way of the sun, everything turns gray, distorted, and cold. We know the sun is there, but we can't sense its reality or feel its beneficial power.

Like a bad seat at a ball game where our view is obstructed, we can hear the sounds, feel some of the excitement, watch others who see clearly and are absorbed in the game, but experience only a helpless sense of detachment.

We can't trust Christ while we're in the shadows.

Christ calls us out of the shadows to see Him as He is. Can you step into the brilliance of His warmth and unrelenting care from the shadow of abuse? Are you tired of being disappointed by others who showed you a distorted view of Christ? Are you ready to experience His consistently true nature for yourself firsthand? At first your view will be challenged by the brightness of the Son, but you will grow accustomed to His glory and find yourself basking in the confidence of His trusted direction in your life.

> *Like a bad seat at a ball game where our view is obstructed, we can hear the sounds, feel some of the excitement, watch others who see clearly and are absorbed in the game, but experience only a helpless sense of detachment.*

It should not go unnoticed that Christ has been a leader to millions over the last two thousand years, and He has never yet betrayed, used, or disappointed those who committed themselves to Him as fully devoted followers. Christ is the time-tested Leader who still calls us to trust Him. Busters need Him. All of us need Him. At the end of life on our own, He remains as the only viable option. The popular song by John Mandeville reflects Christ's role in disenfranchised lives: "Things change, plans fail, . . . Jesus will still be there."

TAKE IT FROM THOSE WHO KNEW HIM BEST

The leadership of Christ in people's lives was so reliable and rewarding that through three intensive years of exposure twenty-four hours a day, people of power, vision, and influence turned their lives over to Him. So compelling was the nature of Christ that after He left, they followed Him for the rest of their lives. And some of them

willingly shed their blood in martyrdom simply because they were
fully devoted followers.

There was obviously something more than intriguing about
Christ. These early followers who had known Him, seen Him, heard
Him, and verified His authenticity unflinchingly turned their lives
over to His control. Whatever resistance we have to becoming non-
negotiated followers pales in the face of the reality of who this Christ
is. It is enough to note that He is the God of the universe, Creator,
Lord over all, and Savior of mankind. Yet beyond that, His right to
call us and lead us has been verified in the real lives of people just like
us—people who struggled with the inner rebellion of their want-tos
and their will, people just like us who feared the vulnerability of losing control, people who had learned to distrust those in authority
over them because they had experienced abuse, misuse, manipulation,
and exploitation. All these people found something different and
unique in Christ. And so will we when we throw our lives at His feet,
look into His face, and say, "Whatever! Just lead me and I will follow!"

Any of us who still think that becoming a fully devoted follower is a sign of weakness need to note that Christ as a leader drew followers who were businessmen, bureaucrats, social revolutionaries,
thoughtful intellects, and financiers. The group even included an
unrepentant skeptic. These were hardly weak people. Though not of
the elite inner circles of society, they were anything but weak, unwill-
ful people with nothing better to do. In fact, He has summoned followers from among the strong and satisfied for centuries. His moral
authority and directives for living have not only been tried and
proven, but through His followers have shaped the course of history and formed the very best elements of the Western culture.

THE COMPELLING CHRIST

We all take our careers seriously. They are the source of our
income and hold the prospect for promotion and recognition.
Careers give us something to wake up for in the morning. They build
within us a sense of worth and contribution. Their pension funds help
secure our future and empower our retirement.

Jesus' early followers had careers. The gospel of Matthew relates that as Christ "was walking beside the Sea of Galilee, he saw two brothers, Simon called Peter and his brother Andrew. They were casting a net into the lake, for they were fishermen."

And they weren't on vacation. Fishing was what they did for a living.

Christ said to them, "Come, follow me . . . and I will make you fishers of men."

We shouldn't be surprised that this one claiming to be the Messiah would call some to follow Him. What is surprising is that "at once they left their nets and followed him" (Matt. 4:18–20).

Imagine giving up your career for someone who made a huge claim yet was someone you hardly knew. His claim and call obviously resonated in their souls. So they followed Him into the face of uncertainty. Christ didn't spread out a road map showing where He would lead them. He never does that. We would like to negotiate a deal and evaluate the small print before we sign on to follow. But followers don't cut deals with Christ. They just follow. It is a relationship that confronts the uncertainty and fear with unflinching trust. For followers, all the question marks fall into line behind Christ, who is the exclamation point.

Christ's next encounter was with another pair of brothers, James and John. They, too, were busy about their careers as fishermen, with the added wrinkle that theirs was a family business. Matthew relates that they were mending their nets in their boat with Zebedee, their father. It's one thing to leave your own business, but to leave the family business is another. Note the response: "And immediately they left the boat and their father and followed him" (4:22).

Christ didn't spread out a road map showing where
He would lead His followers. He never does that.

And then there came Nathaniel, Thomas, Philip, Simon the Zealot, Matthew, Judas, and two more.

What made these men so ready for a midstream correction in their lives, particularly one as radical as this? I wonder if it had ever crossed their minds that there may be more to life than the piles of fish that they harvested from the sea or that being a wealthy bureaucrat was not all it was cracked up to be. One was a member of the local resistance force plotting to overthrow the oppressive Roman regime. Did he despair that his once ripe dreams of overthrowing Rome had died on the vine, or was it that he saw this movement as the means whereby his political aspirations could finally be realized? Did Thomas, the unrepentant skeptic, finally find someone to trust? Was it a sense of Christ's transparent purity and untainted vision that compelled Nathaniel, a guileless idealist, to follow? And what of Judas, the trusted financier—what could ever have motivated him?

Perhaps it was that the national demise of Israel had spawned a deepening sense of despondency, cynicism, and despair. Their once proud nation that had been favored of God was now under the oppressive dominion of the pagan Roman Empire. Their own leaders had conspired with the occupiers for financial gain, prominence, and safety. Even the religious establishment of their day had long lost its sense of ministry. The least of the citizens was forced to carry the weight of imposed tradition under the watchful eyes of proud and self-righteous spiritual leaders who themselves were in league with the foreign political system.

Such was the scene when Christ came. These men were familiar, through the centuries-old literature and archives, with the long-hoped-for promises of One who would come and be greater than their greatest leaders of past centuries. Prophets had told of a Messiah who would execute justice and righteousness on the earth (Jer. 33:15–16). If their predictions were right, this Messiah would restore their once proud nation to all its former glory and more. More than that, He would offer personal peace and satisfaction.

All these factors—factors that correspond to our world today—no doubt merged in the hearts and minds of these early followers. From the gnawing sense of meaninglessness to the despair of an unraveling society, we have yet to find a point of certainty in which we can hope. We, too, are looking for something or someone above and beyond ourselves to give life meaning and purpose.

But the reason that these fishermen and others were ready to follow Christ is largely speculation. Bonhoeffer points out that Scripture is silent about the psychological and societal realities that may have been behind their prompt responsiveness to Christ's call. The reason for the silence, he suggests, is that those realities were not the important, primary reasons.

> Unfortunately our text is ruthlessly silent on this point, and in fact it regards the immediate sequence of call and response as a matter of crucial importance. It displays not the slightest interest in the psychological reasons for man's religious decisions. And why? For the simple reason that the cause behind the immediate following of call by response is Jesus Christ himself. It is Jesus who calls, and because it is Jesus, Levi follows at once. This encounter is a testimony to the absolute, direct, and unaccountable authority of Jesus. There is no need of any preliminaries, and no other consequence but obedience to the call. Because Jesus is the Christ, he has the authority to call and to demand obedience to his word. Jesus summons men to follow him not as a teacher or a pattern of a good life, but as the Christ, the Son of God.[3]

While following Christ does not always mean—as it did for the disciples—leaving our careers, it will mean radically altering our view of them. It is a potent reflection of the compelling nature of Christ that seasoned, successful men, who were leaders in their own right, would in the end rather follow Him than their own dreams and aspirations—at great personal cost. Where do we see such dedication today?

> *While following Christ does not always mean—*
> *as it did for the disciples—leaving our careers,*
> *it will mean radically altering our view of them.*

Randy Robinson is a gifted plastic surgeon who specializes in dental and craniofacial surgery. He oversees a thriving clinic in Denver with several partners. But Randy's heart beats for more than professional recognition and an affluent lifestyle. The mainspring of his life—and therefore his work—is his relationship with Christ. He is a true follower, one who has asked the question, What would Christ have me do with the skills He has given me?

The answer led Randy to the jungles of Vietnam, where many children and young people are so grotesquely deformed from the long-term effects of war, disease, genetic defects, environmental hazards, and other traumas that Westerners would gasp just to look at them. In most cases the damage is functional more than cosmetic: eyes that cannot see, noses that cannot smell, ears that cannot hear, fingers that cannot grasp, feet that cannot walk. Randy took with him a team of medical personnel and as many supplies as they could muster, and for days they operated out of a provincial "hospital"—little more than a shack by American standards. Conditions were so spare that the team had to sterilize their instruments with little more than boiling water and alcohol and even had to reuse sutures to stitch up their patients. Fans helped to keep the doctors and nurses from fainting as they operated in stifling heat and humidity. And a leaky pump on one piece of equipment poured anesthetic into the air, making the doctors woozy.

But in the name of Christ, Randy's team brought hope to boys and girls who otherwise had no hope. For one, they repaired a cleft palette. For another, they removed tissue that had caused the face to swell all out of proportion. For another, they pulled an eye around from the side of the face to the front. In addition, they administered vaccinations, gave checkups, diagnosed ailments, and prescribed regimens of treatment.

Instructed by the Communist government not to speak publicly about the gospel, Randy and his team nevertheless let it be known through private conversations just why they had come to Vietnam and Who stood behind their efforts. As a result, the name of Jesus spread quickly through the region.

After more such trips to Vietnam and South America, Randy and his wife, Ginger, organized Face the Challenge, a nonprofit ministry dedicated to providing state-of-the-art craniofacial surgery in some of the poorest places in the world—in the name of Christ. As a result of their commitment to follow, they are having an incredible impact for Christ in the Third World.

THE ULTIMATE CHARISMATIC LEADER

Decades ago, the father of modern management philosophy, social scientist Max Weber (1864–1920), theorized three ideal types of leadership. They were legal (a president who is vested with authority by a legal or constitutional system), authoritarian (a dictator who by sheer force of his power can control and lead), and charismatic.[4]

The common idea of a charismatic leader is one who leads with charm and personality, but that was not Weber's definition. In Weber's view, charismatic leaders stand outside the regular forms of authority and come to the fore in times of social upheaval to fill the vacuum with their vision.

Weber proposed that the charismatic leader was the most unusual of the three and the only one "who might counter the dispiriting effects of life in an overly bureaucratic and rationalistic world," what he called "the iron cage of modernity." It was Weber's hope, in fact, that such a leader, "endowed with extraordinary, even superhuman qualities might be able to instill in his followers a sense of mission and moral purpose that a thoroughly demystified society no longer provides."[5]

Christ is the One whom Weber was looking for. Could it have been Weber's heart's longing that was being expressed amid his sociological rhetoric? Endowed with authority by the God of the universe, Jesus comes into this world of broken expectations, standing quite apart from any temporal authority, and rises out of the ashes of a despairing society and our despondent lives to offer a fresh view of life and new hope to all who will follow Him.

If you had been Thomas or Peter or any other disciple and you believed that this was the One who had finally come to fulfill all your inner longings and establish stability in your world, you may have left your nets as well. If you had heard the incarnate God of the universe call you face-to-face, you would have impulsively obeyed. That word "Me" in His call to "Follow Me" is what makes unconditional followership so compelling. It is a compelling call because He is a compelling Person.

*That word "Me" in His call to "Follow Me" is what
makes unconditional followership so compelling. It is a
compelling call because He is a compelling person.*

Christ not only fills the emptiness with significance but also leads us in lifeways that, unlike the pagan paths, are stable, certain, and successful. He said, "I have come that they may have life, and have it to the full" (John 10:10).

When Christ promised this, He was not necessarily speaking in temporal, external, or material measures of abundance. His offer of life is far deeper and more expansive in every way than piles of possessions and the fleeting pleasures of life. Nor does followership mean that life may not be abundantly blessed with piles and pleasure. Indeed, some of the most devoted followers of Christ have been profoundly supplied with much. All this simply goes to say Christ never measures life by the benefits but rather by the essence of life in the long view. And the essence of life and the long view demand that we have Christ at the center of life as the singular pursuit of existence.

THAT PERSONAL TOUCH

Perhaps our struggle to fully embrace Christ as leader relates to the fact that we feel that we are, in effect, merely "grandstand Christians." While Christ has indeed done spectacular things for others that validate His claim to lead, He really hasn't done all that much for us. A cognitive, ritualistic, distant relationship with Christ rarely cultivates good soil for followership. It's the real encounters with this Leader that make Him so compelling. It's His personal touch that convinces us of the value and worth of this relationship.

I felt the tension when the Brooklyn Tabernacle Choir opened its concert at Moody's 1996 Founder's Week. As the lights dimmed and the spotlights came on, I noticed early into the first number that tears were glistening on many faces in the choir. These are not professional musicians but regular church choir members who had come to Chicago to minister to us. As these 180 voices praised the God of their liberation, their tears communicated that they had experienced very real personal encounters with Christ. I thought of how many of them had been rescued from life in the bowels of Brooklyn, of what a glorious ascent it must have been for them to be redeemed. For them, Christ is more than just an intellectual arrangement guaranteeing their eternity. He is more than just a piece of their lives—He is the compelling reality of their existence. He is One whom they can gladly follow.

Quite frankly, at that moment I felt that I had been cheated. I came to Christ when I was six years old, so my deliverance was from things like biting my sister and not picking up my toys. Then it struck me that if Christ never does anything more than redeem me, He has already done far more than I deserve. Eternity will prove what a compelling encounter that truly is.

I pondered what might have been: Where might I be today if He hadn't reached down to that little boy in Hackensack, New Jersey, and touched him with His marvelous grace? Where might my greed, lusts, self-centeredness, and impetuosity have taken me if all my life they hadn't been checked by the persistent pressure of the indwelling Spirit? What might have come of my life, my relationships, my sense of wholeness if life had been permitted to freelance without restraint? It was then that I knew that I had been blessed with a strategic personal encounter with Christ.

So why wouldn't I follow Him? Whom else would I follow if I didn't follow Him?

And just in case you think that He hasn't done anything for you lately, remember how active He is every day, keeping out anything that would be more than you can bear (1 Cor. 10:13) and prohibiting anything that He cannot turn to glory and gain (Rom. 8:28; James 1:2–5). Putting our heads on the pillow at night should be an exercise in ecstatic gratitude for the fact that Christ and His angels have been busy on our behalf, guarding and guiding us all the way through the day and guaranteeing that we cannot be fatally damaged by an adversary who seeks to destroy us.

THE POWER OF UNDAUNTED DEVOTION

To commit ourselves to Christ as fully devoted followers, we must be struck not just with the benefits of our encounters with Him but also with the divine authority of the Person we are following and the cause to which He leads us. As we have noted, following is simply a matter of unqualified obedience to the incarnate God of the universe. If benefits alone were the motivation, the followers of the first century would have bailed out immediately, since for many of them, to follow meant being marginalized, maligned, and sometimes martyred. Both Christ and His cause were so compelling that they were followers regardless. This is the kind of followership to which we must aspire. And while most of us will never be called to follow to the shedding of our blood, or for that matter not even to a measure of their sacrifice, it is still unconditional followership that Christ both demands and deserves.

Followers in the first century were not above the temptation to follow Christ for all the wrong reasons. Scripture relates that after the feeding of the five thousand, the crowd followed Christ across the sea the next day to see if He would feed them again. He sternly rebuked their stomach-first motivation for following and refused to do another miracle to satisfy misplaced affection.

Judas is a mirror reflection of those who follow Christ for the perks. As soon as his financial aspirations were not realized and the prospect of some suffering became evident, he was gone, putting Christ's life in jeopardy and suffering the deep regret that emerged from doing life his way.

But the rest of the disciples would have died for Christ. Some of them did. They placed all their hopes and dreams for their future in His hands without negotiation. And they were not disappointed—at least not in the long haul. They were fully devoted followers. Although they were at times imperfect followers, they nevertheless remained undaunted in their commitment to continue to follow Him.

They were fully devoted followers, even
though at times they were imperfect followers.

They were so effective in their followership that, as we have noted, their influence ultimately led to the surrender of the Roman

Empire. An entire civilization was forged that for centuries would be based upon Christ's ways and reflect His justice and righteousness in its law. Its mores and its greatest music, art, and literature, would be born out of the foundational teachings of this One whom they followed. This was all because followers showed their world the reality of Christ as the unconditional Leader of their lives.

This same Leader calls us to follow Him.

He is the compelling Christ. When we see Him clearly and realize that His marvelous grace touches us in every hour of our lives, we have to ask, "Why wouldn't we follow Him?"

Who would we follow if we didn't follow Him? Would we really want to ignore Him and follow our own instincts, knowing as we do what happens when we live for ourselves?

CHAPTER SIX

IT'S A PERSONAL THING

The Pleasure and Power of Intimacy with Christ

Ernest Hemingway, the literary genius, said this about his life: "I live in a vacuum that is as lonely as a radio tube when the batteries are dead, and there is no current to plug into."

This is a startling statement, given the fact that Hemingway lived his life in a way that would be the envy of any person who had bought the values of our modern society. Hemingway was known for his tough-guy image and globe-trotting pilgrimages to exotic and far-away places. He was a big-game hunter, a bullfighter, a man who could drink the best of them under the table. He was married four times and lived his life seemingly without moral restraint or conscience. But on a sunny Sunday morning in Idaho, he pulverized his head with a shotgun blast.

Not only does Hemingway stand as a symbol of the bankruptcy of a self-managed life, but he also models for us another reality that very few people know about. Ernest Hemingway grew up in a solid evangelical Christian home in Oak Park, Illinois. His grandparents were missionaries, and his father was a devoted churchman and best of friends with evangelist Dwight Lyman Moody. Hemingway's family conformed to the strictest codes of Christianity, and as a boy and young man Hemingway was active in the life of his church, serving as a choirboy.

Then came the First World War, and Hemingway went away as a war correspondent and saw the death and despair that only a war like that can bring. His youthful enthusiasm for Christianity was soured to the point where he progressively, through the next several years, rejected his upbringing and denied the validity and credibility of the Christ that he once had embraced.

Or had he?

While we certainly don't know all that transpired, it would seem fair to say that Ernest Hemingway never developed a truly personal relationship with Christ. Living in an environment, going through catechism, conforming to the codes, and expressing a general affirmation of the truths of Scripture are not really what genuine Christianity consists of. Authentic Christianity is composed of non-negotiated followers who are progressively moving toward Christ and who understand all of life and all of this world in the context of His teaching and His truth. If we aren't cultivating a living, vital relationship with Jesus Christ, then we, too, can respond as Hemingway did when either life's questions are agonizingly unanswerable or when our inner impulses are too seductive for us to resist. Relating to systems, rituals, and rules as a point of allegiance is never enough to keep us unflinchingly loyal.

The point really is not Hemingway's life. It's my life and your life. The point is whether we are simply fellow travelers along for the ride for reasons other than Christ, or are genuinely pursuing a relationship with Him.

The point is whether we are simply fellow travelers
along for the ride for reasons other than Christ, or are
genuinely pursuing a relationship with Him.

WOULD YOU KNOW A FOLLOWER IF YOU SAW ONE?

Scripture is crystal clear about the profile of a true follower of Jesus Christ. Interestingly, in the text in Matthew 4 that recounts the call of Christ to Andrew, Peter, James, and John, a different word is used for their response to Christ than the word that Christ used to call them. As we have seen, Christ's call means that we are to "come after Him." The essence of that call involves the direction of our lives.

The word that characterized the disciples' response, however, was full of additional meaning. It was a technical word used of individuals in that day who were known by their friends and others around them as followers. According to linguistic scholars, it reflected two basic nuances. First, a follower was one who had a growing and deepening relationship to the one they were following. Followers do not characterize their following as a task or project or duty. It is, as we have already noted, first and foremost a relationship to this person who is being followed. Second, a true follower is in the process of a radical reformation because of the influence of the leader on his life. True followers do not remain the same once they start following Christ. He is involved in a task of radical reformation in our lives in terms of both character and conduct. Followers become imitators of the one they are following. You know a follower because he acts and reacts like the one who is leading his life.

So in the time of the disciples, someone who called you a follower of Christ would expect to see your life busy about relationship and reformation.

This identity was so clear in Christ's day that calling someone a follower would be no different from saying of someone, "He's a trucker" or "She's a doctor." It defined the privilege and responsibility of their role as followers. It spoke volumes about who they were and explained why they lived, thought, and acted as they did.

Coming to understand what it means to be identified as a follower in specific, life-related terms is imperative if we are to actualize the privilege of becoming fully devoted followers of Christ whose lives are marked by relationship and reformation.

RELATIONSHIP

The word for "follow" applied to Peter, Andrew, James, and John in Matthew 4:19–21 indicates a person who so longed to know the right way to live that he initiated a relationship with the local rabbi, knowing that the rabbi was the very epitome of God's truth about life as expressed in the Torah. The Torah contained God's revealed definitions and directives for life. It was God's means of managing instincts toward what was not only productive and good, but also toward what would bring glory to Him and gain to His plans and purposes. Followers in the rabbinical sense were those who had so longed for God and His standards that they moved in with the local rabbi as a means of knowing and growing toward God. The closest you could get to God on earth was through the rabbi. So followers in the technical sense were those who attached themselves to the local rabbi. These individuals often left everything they owned to live with the rabbi. They would serve the rabbi, sit at his feet, watch him intently, and seek, by following him, to go where their longing for life in God's way could be satisfied.

This New Testament word for "following," C. Blendinger notes, involves identifying so intimately with the one being followed that we incorporate our lives with his. He describes this as an innate relationship of rational man with God. He describes the relationship of a follower to the rabbi in these terms:

> The words describe the relationship of a pupil to a teacher of the Torah. The pupil who chooses to subordinate himself to a Rabbi follows him everywhere he goes, learning from him and above all serving him. The pupil's obligation to serve is an essential part of learning the Law. The goal of all his learning and training is a complete knowledge of the Torah, and ability to practice it in every situation.[1]

The follower in Christ's day was clearly marked as one who had a personal relationship with the local rabbi. And the relationship was the preeminent reality of his or her life.

Christ is the local rabbi of our souls. Moreover, He personalizes our relationship with Him by initiating an interest in us. He not only initiated a divinely authoritative call in our lives, but also bought us with the price of His own life on the cross. He lures us with persistent love into a deepening relationship with Him. He is God, and a relationship with Him literally explodes with the love and leadership that we long for.

> *Following is, at the very heart of it all, a*
> *relationship with One who highly values intimacy*
> *with us and works to enable and empower it.*

And, thankfully, He doesn't lead us down well-worn, conventional paths that we have long been accustomed to. Relating to this Rabbi is an adventure in wisdom that is freshly alive and rewardingly different.

Through all the pilgrimage He loves us—regardless. He loves us all the way home to heaven. He could and would never say to us, "I didn't ask you to follow, so don't bother Me with your problems. If it doesn't work out, you can go back where you came from." Following is, at the very heart of it all, a relationship with One who highly values intimacy with us and works to enable and empower it. I'm reminded of the words of St. Augustine: "Thou askest what thou shouldst offer for thee? Offer thyself. For what else doth the Lord seek of thee but thee? Because of all the creatures, he hath made nothing better than thee. He seekest thyself from thyself."[2]

For us then, following means to adopt Him as the local rabbi of our lives and surrender; to sit under His wisdom in order to learn from Him; and to serve Him in every way possible. It means to give Him the highest priority as the supreme relationship of life out of which every other relationship and activity is defined and directed.

GETTING TO KNOW HIM

Turning fifty, as I did recently, was a real wake-up call for me. I realized anew how much ground I still have to gain in my personal relationship with Christ. After years of the fast-paced, hectic business of serving Him, I confess that I've spent far more time *doing for* Him than *getting to know* Him.

I figure I have one more high-energy run in which to maximize my life for Him. And I find that in the deepest part of my being, I want this season to be marked by a followership that springs from a deepening intimacy with Christ.

If you like fishing, you know that casting a line toward the shore and pulling it back is essentially what it's all about. It is not the activity of going through that routine that counts, but rather, how you do it. If the line is pulled back quickly, it covers a lot of territory but simply skims the surface. If you slow down as you retrieve, it goes deeper and deeper, where presumably the fish are.

I have an unquenchable desire to slow down and find my life going deeper in my walk with Christ. I want to meet Him in the depths of my soul, away from the stress and press of everything on top. A relationship with Christ is the key to fulfilling our deepest longings. We were built for a relationship with God. All of life is about searching to fill the void that sin and separation from Him have created within. Filling the emptiness with piles of things, earthly friendships, satisfying experiences, and sensual encounters ultimately proves to achieve less than what we had hoped for. Christ is the only one who fits. It's just a matter of finding a way to successfully get in touch with Him and let Him fill the space.

Without a doubt, at the core of every believer's life is a longing to know more of Him—to relate more fully, more experientially with Him. There is a reason that the book *Experiencing God* has sold over a million copies. We all want to say, with the psalmist,

> As the deer pants for streams of water,
> so my soul pants for you, O God.
> My soul thirsts for God, for the living God.
> When can I go and meet with God?

> (Ps. 42:1–2)

> O God, you are my God,
> earnestly I seek you;

my soul thirsts for you,
   my body longs for you,
in a dry and weary land
   where there is no water.

(Ps. 63:1)

We want to experience Him.

But moving from the desire to deepen our relationship to actually doing it is the challenge. Developing an experiential, personal relationship with Christ often seems to be the elusive dream of our faith. We've talked about such a relationship our whole Christian life, assumed that we have had one, and then wondered why it wasn't all we thought it would be. After a brief sensation of warmth when we first met Christ, we quickly lost the glow and Christianity became increasingly routine. We grew accustomed to Him and the sound of His anthems and sermons. Service for Him was an important part of our experience, but it, too, was a task rarely fulfilling unless we got a personal rush through affirmation, position, or power. We are good Christians and do the Christian thing, but never seem to experience the intimacy with Christ that we long for.

The experience is like working for a company where the benefits are the very best available. We execute our daily work. We enjoy the regular paychecks. We join with our colleagues to help solve problems through teamwork. We applaud our owner and CEO in employee assemblies and almost feel a kinship with him. We read the manuals he has written for us and find ourselves curiously drawn to him. But he never shows up. He was seen a long time ago but not recently. So we are disappointed—not because we don't want to work for him, but because we understood that the boss wants to get to know us. Yet no one has told us where he is. The radiance and glow of their lives seem to indicate that they have found him, but we find ourselves still looking, wanting, waiting.

In the book *The Superman Syndrome,* Jack Kuhatschek writes, "Many Christians today have a hunger to experience God. In fact, many of us were attracted to Christ in the first place because we were told that we would have a 'personal relationship' with him. Yet if we are honest, we must confess that it is very different from any other relationship we have ever known."[3]

Think of the frustration of being designed for, redeemed toward, and enticed to have a relationship with someone who is invisible and untouchable. This is the most unique aspect of a relationship with Christ, yet it is, when we understand it, its greatest advantage. Understanding a personal relationship with Christ begins by realizing that it is a supernatural, nonmaterial experience. We are so locked into earthly material experiences that we don't easily appreciate the higher form of the world that is above, around, and in us. In fact, we often speak of this flat touchable place where we live as the real world—as though the world of Christ and the Spirit is not the real thing or real only in some distant, irrelevant way.

A personal relationship with Christ is found in His *world.*
That's where He resides and where He will be found.

The real world is not this upside-down, fallen sphere that is controlled and manipulated by our adversary. This is the short-lived, condemned world where truth and reality are contradicted and sometimes despised. The real world is Christ's eternal home, to which we have been redeemed and permanently assigned (Col. 1:13). It is now. It is composed of His presence, heaven's culture, His body, and it is authentically expressed and validated by His people, the church. A personal relationship with Christ is found in *His* world. That's where He resides and where He will be found.

Relating to a God who is invisible yet real—and really with us—is a benefit not a drawback. When you think of it, it is often the material aspects of relationships that create problems. People may look intimidating or, by contrast, wimpishly self-effacing. Friends aren't always there when we need them. False expectations and misunderstandings arise from physical, verbal, and material connections in a relationship. For the real, risen, transcendent, ever-present resident Christ to relate to me in the very depths of my being apart from the inherent trappings of visibility is an advantage with which no earthly relationship can compare. As we shall see, there are indeed physical aspects to our relationship that complement our spiritual experience with Christ.

*How do I transition from a dutiful,
distant, one-sided relationship with Christ to
experience a deepening intimacy with Him?*

Christ noted this advantage—the invisible aspects of our relationship—when He sought to comfort His traumatized followers after He broke the news that He was leaving. They had staked their lives on His presence. They had given up everything for Him and risked all on a hoped-for future with Him. Yet after three short years, He was going to leave for reasons they could not fully understand. He told them it was going to be better for them because He would send the Spirit to them. And, He said, it is better because "I was *with* you and He will be *in* you." The distinct advantage for us is that we are linked twenty-four hours a day to God in the person of the indwelling Spirit. This Spirit enables us to know, understand, and respond in ways that please Christ and, more importantly, put us in touch with the person of Christ. As Christ said,

> I will ask the Father, and he will give you another Counselor to be with you forever—the Spirit of truth. The world cannot accept him, because it neither sees him nor knows him. But you know him, for he lives with you and will be in you. . . .
> But I tell you the truth: It is for your good that I am going away. Unless I go away, the Counselor will not come to you; but if I go, I will send him to you. . . .
> But when he, the Spirit of truth, comes, he will guide you into all truth. He will not speak on his own; he will speak only what he hears, and he will tell you what is yet to come. He will bring glory to me by taking from what is mine and making it known to you. All that belongs to the Father is mine. That is why I said the Spirit will take from what is mine and make it known to you.
>
> *John 14:16–17; 16:7, 13–15*

The question remains: How do I transition from a dutiful, distant, one-sided relationship with Christ to experience a deepening intimacy with Him?

DISCIPLINES OF THE HEART

There are at least six disciplines in our lives that will cultivate the ground of our hearts for growing a personal experience with Him.

1. Open the door of your heart. Perhaps the most important aspect of our pursuit of Christ is the realization that He wants and pursues a personal relationship with us. In the ancient world, eating together was the ultimate expression of fellowship and friendship. Inviting someone in to eat expressed a desire to have a deeper relationship. Revelation 3:20 is often thought of as an invitation to our salvation experience, but the verse actually speaks to Christ's persistent desire for intimacy with His followers. He pictures Himself as knocking at the door of our hearts, wanting to come in: "Here I am! I stand at the door and knock." And He gives us this assurance: "If anyone hears my voice and opens the door, I will come in and eat with him, and he with me."

Where is Christ? Standing at the door, waiting for me to take the initiative to welcome Him to a relationship that He longs to have with me.

It is our heart's door. This is the pivotal issue. If we do not comprehend this, we will not get to know Him personally.

In Scripture we discover that our heart is where we dream, deliberate, decide, want, and will. It is Control Central. It is the only fully independent entity in our entire existence. No one invades it unless we give permission. It is the core of who and what we are. It is the real, authentic me. After all the layers of the external camouflage have been removed, my heart is the naked reality of what I really am.

This is the place where Christ wants to meet us, and He won't meet us anywhere else. We want to meet Him at church, in our quiet time, at the safe and comfortable outer edges of what we pretend to be. But He meets us in our hearts. If it is intimacy we want, then the relationship must happen where intimacy happens. Christ is not interested in relating to the masks and the costumes. He's not into camouflage. He wants to know and fellowship with the real me.

And we can be thankful for that.

Yet it is an unsettling thought. If He comes to meet me there . . .

- He finds things that He will want to get rid of right away: that pleasure, that habit, that long-standing bitterness, etc., etc., etc.
- He will want to be in charge of my desires, decisions, wants, and will. He is the sovereign God of the universe and rightfully holds complete authority.
- He will notice the clutter of irrelevancies and trivia.
- He will see me as I really am, including my fears about my lack of worth and dignity.

Christ is not interested in relating to the masks and the costumes. He's not into camouflage. He wants to know and fellowship with the real me.

Regardless of all that, He will still come in—gladly. He will work through the issues in a patient and persistent partnership until the air starts to clear with the purity, power, and pleasure of His presence. He will redecorate our hearts and transform them into a showplace for Him, an image that captivates C. S. Lewis:

I find I must borrow yet another parable from George MacDonald. Imagine yourself as a living house. God comes in to rebuild that house. At first, perhaps, you can understand what He is doing. He is getting the drains right and stopping the leaks in the roof and so on: you knew that those jobs needed doing and so you are not surprised. But presently he starts knocking the house about in a way that hurts abominably and does not seem to make sense. What on earth is He up to? The explanation is that He is building quite a different house from the one you thought of—throwing out a new wing here, putting on an extra floor there, running up towers, making courtyards. You thought you were going to be made into a decent little cottage:

but He is building a palace. He intends to come and live in it Himself.[4]

Experiencing a personal relationship with Christ requires that I consciously welcome Him into my heart. It starts when I yield full control of my desires and decisions to His presence and give Him the right He deserves to do deep cleaning and major remodeling if necessary. It means praying the welcoming plea that David did:

> *Search me, O God, and know my heart;*
> *test me and know my anxious thoughts.*
> *See if there is any offensive way in me,*
> *and lead me in the way everlasting.*
>
> (Ps. 139:23–24)

There can be no compromise here. Either Christ comes in as Lord of all my heart, or He doesn't come in. If He doesn't come in, I won't experience the pleasure of His presence. He will still be with me and will ultimately take me home. But if it's a relationship I'm hungry for, then I have to let Him in. And I must not be afraid. Whatever He does will be done in loving consistency. He is there because He loves me. Every heart that has opened to Him is better by far for doing so.

2. Pursue Him. Relationships are built on communication and closeness. We cannot neglect regular conversations through prayer and exposure to His Word. Study His patterns of attitude, action, and reaction in the Gospels. Ask Him the tough questions and stay close until He starts to sort things out for you. Meditate on and memorize both His Word and the works of His hands, whether in the world around you, in the lives of others, or in your own life.

Practice praise and worship for His character, wisdom, intriguing perspectives, and anything else that you either embrace by faith or experience personally. As He promises, "The LORD inhabits the praises of His people." Praise Him all day long in creative ways, both in the warmth and quiet of your heart and in the public square. Celebrate Him with God's people, expressing the reality of this deepening intimacy you are experiencing.

3. Put Him in His place. Make it your heart's desire that He is at the center of everything you do. As the sun is to the solar system, so the Savior is to the life of one who passionately pursues Him. Everything is illuminated, measured, and defined by His place in the preeminent center. Expel self, money, success, friends, pleasure, power and position, comfort and convenience, and anything else that usurps His place in the center. Put Him finally and forever there. Sincerely repent for relegating the Son to the secondary role of a "planet" revolving around whatever we have wrongly placed at the center.

4. Be where He is. We don't relate to Christ on our terms. He never gets off track in order to fellowship with us where we have strayed. Calling, "Lord, I'm over here in my bitterness and self-centeredness. Come! What would you like with your tea?" really doesn't cut it if we are pursuing a personal relationship with Him. We find Him where *He* is, and fellowship means being there with Him. We fellowship with Him in acts of love, justice, mercy, humility, forgiveness, and righteousness. We experience His joy and power as we faithfully serve Him because we love Him. Serving others with acts of generosity and compassion puts us in close proximity to Him.

*We don't relate to Christ on our terms. We find Him
where* He *is, and fellowship means being there with Him.*

In experiencing Christ, distance is damaging. Absence does *not* make the heart grow fonder. Keep short accounts on sin. Develop a sensitivity to where He is and where He is working. *Be* there. And train your heart to know when you are starting to follow afar off.

5. Meet Him in the crisis. Seldom do we have a better opportunity to experience Christ personally than those times when we face a wrenching crisis. In the bad times He shows most clearly His grace, power, wisdom, and sustaining presence. Resisting or avoiding the crisis keeps us from experiencing Him as fully as we can. Shadrach, Meshach, and Abednego knew their God more intimately after their ordeal in the fiery furnace than before. (Ironically, it was their unconditional obedience that caused their problem in the first place.)

Because of his obedience in a time of crisis, Moses was able to do something he never thought he could. After leading the people of Israel from Egypt, he knew the reality of His God and fellowshipped in that relationship for the rest of his life.

6. See Him in His people. Although He is not visible, Christ manifests Himself through His people as they interact in the reality of the character, actions, and attitudes of His presence within. A widow told me that when someone comforted her with a hug, "It was like the arms of God around my life." While Christ is invisible, His body the church is visible and as such manifests His reality and presence. A hand that gives to us is His hand. A word that is encouraging, comforting, or confronting is His voice to us. An act of love, companionship, or compassion is His touch on our lives.

Sally lay awake in her room, afraid of what might be lurking in the dark. Her father came into her room several times to tell her that the Lord was there with her and that she had nothing to fear. Finally, in desperation she replied to her dad's theology, "I know, but I want somethin' that has skin on it!"

Bobby knelt by his bed just before Christmas to say his bedtime prayers with his mother. He mumbled through the rote prayer "Now I lay me . . ." and then blurted out, "and, Lord, you know how much I want a bicycle for Christmas!"

To which his mom said, "Shhh! God's not deaf."

"I know, but Grandma is."

And while we don't recommend that kind of manipulative approach to experiencing Christ's provision through His body, I think Bobby understood the concept.

> *What a change we would see in the fellowship of*
> *believers if we would all commit ourselves to being*
> *His hands, feet, heart, and voice to those around us.*

What a change we would see in the fellowship of believers if we would all commit ourselves to being His hands, feet, heart, and voice to those around us. It would be particularly powerful if we resisted the urge to seek recognition for well doing and instead emphasized that it was the reality of Christ that was blessing people's lives.

We the people are His presence.

Six principles of intimacy emerge:

- Christ wants to come in to our lives through the door of our hearts. Followers take the initiative to welcome Him within.
- Christ stands ready to be found and known in prayer, His Word, and His active work in our lives and the world around us. Followers find Him in these privileged practices.
- Christ's presence is experienced when He is at the strategic center of all we are and do. Followers put Him there.
- Christ relates to us in the sphere of who He is, where He is, what He is, and what He wants to do. Followers meet Him in these unusual places.
- Christ often leads us into and through crisis situations so that we become convinced of His reality and presence in our lives. Followers view crises as opportunities to experience Him more fully.
- Christ meets us, speaks to us, and touches us through the physical and visible reality of His body the church. Followers look for Him there.

The development and the discipline of these principles create the capacity for an authentically experienced personal relationship with Christ.

THE MORAL MUSCLE OF A FOLLOWER

The issue of relationship is strategically central to our success as followers. Rarely will one deny himself for a system or an institution. But often we will deny ourselves to preserve the priority of a valued relationship.

The book of Genesis relates the story of Joseph, who as a young man was sold into slavery in Egypt. Rising to power in a wealthy government official's household, Joseph was placed in charge of all the estate. Potiphar's wife—who no doubt was one of the pick of the land, given her husband's position and power—sought repeatedly to seduce Joseph. Think of Joseph, who—in the prime of his sexuality, having been betrayed by his own brothers and placed far away from any family restraint—must now reach for something deep enough and strong enough to fend off these sensual advances. It was hardly going to do for him to "just say no" or to remind himself of the rules his father taught him as a boy. Those restraints may have been enough that first and second time she approached him. But Potiphar's wife pursued him day after day and still he resisted. Where does such character come from? What's the secret?

Joseph finally told her his secret: "With me in charge, . . . my master does not concern himself with anything in the house; everything he owns he has entrusted to my care. . . . My master has withheld nothing from me except you, because you are his wife. How then could I do such a wicked thing and sin against God?" (Gen. 39:8–9). Joseph found strength in valued relationships. Therefore he had the will not to violate his trusted relationship with his boss nor, more importantly, his valued relationship with God.

I find this fascinating because both the Old Testament and the teachings of Christ emphasize that the most important ethic of a successful life is not the memorization and mastery of codified lists of behavioral patterns, but the cultivation of a commitment to "love the Lord your God with all your heart" and "love your neighbor as yourself" (Matt. 22:37, 39). Christ stated that if we were to do these two things, all of the law would automatically fall into place in our lives. Keep in mind that the law was focused to help us manage and direct our passions toward good and godly ends. Our relationship to God and His Son Christ is the motivational key.

The point is that God structured the pattern for restraint in the form of strategic and meaningful relationships. Joseph's moral character was grounded in a commitment to a loving relationship with God and with Potiphar. A set of rules is rarely worth denying our passions their pleasure; valued relationships are always worth self-denial. This is what sets authentic Christianity apart from other religious systems and philosophies. Christianity is first and foremost a relationship—a relationship with Christ as the defining and motivating reality of followership.

I recall many occasions when I would have been easy prey to my urges except for the offense that would be to Christ my leader, not to mention the negative effects on my wife, children, friends, and other trusted relationships with students, colleagues, and constituents. A life that isolates itself from meaningful relationships is morally at risk. A life that has not cultivated a personal relationship with Christ is particularly vulnerable.

> *A life that isolates itself from*
> *meaningful relationships is morally at risk.*

Having few valued relationships leaves us with little reason to deny ourselves. This accounts in some measure for the rapid deterioration of the moral fabric of American society. We have valued a kind of individualism that fosters isolation. We have told each other that the only thing that really counts is individual happiness. We construe unhappiness as reasonable grounds for divorce, abortion, indebtedness, sexual experimentation, and a slew of other unguided urges that will further alienate us from God and other people. We live in a society full of people who live in a ghetto of one. More and more, we choose to cultivate technological relationships in cyberspace. And the more apart we feel, the more we seek to satisfy ourselves in destructive patterns that distance us even further from the protective cover of treasured relationships.

Satan's very first attack on mankind drew Eve away from God into isolation. Satan appealed to her individual rights and potential personal advance and used slander to tempt her. Isolated from God and consumed with herself, she gave no thought to her relationship with Adam until after she ate—and then regretted what she had done. The rest is history.

True followership moves in exactly the opposite direction from Eve's. Followers of Christ suppress their instinct for instant gratification in favor of the deeper pleasure of a growing relationship with Him. This in turn puts us in a special union with others who follow Him. Followership is about consecrating ourselves to a growing relationship with Christ, which then provides the resource for the radical reformation that will make me all I should be.

The sequence of the call underlines the pattern of the process. First we follow Him: That is a consuming, relational event. Then He will make us fishers of men: That is radical reformation. It is His intention to transform followers. In the same way we follow an interior decorator to refurbish our house, we follow Christ to experience significant and satisfying change.

We have all seen people who from a distance seem to be compelling. We would like to know them and develop a relationship with them. It was like that when I fell in love with my wife, Martie.

I can remember seeing Martie for the first time when she was a college freshman. I noticed her just a week or so after we had all arrived on campus, and each time I saw her there was something intriguing about her, even though it was from a distance. Soon I got the courage to ask for her company for an evening, and she agreed. The more I got to know her, the more compelling a person she became. And it wasn't long until I was wanting a full-time, lifelong relationship with her. And when the big question was asked, she said yes. She is no doubt the most compelling person in my life—and I have been following her for nearly thirty years now.

I do not continue to live with Martie only because of vows or commitments I have made. Although they are vitally important and would keep me in the relationship if they were all that was left, I'm not in this for the "institution" of marriage. I don't continue to live with Martie just because it's the respectable thing to do and people will think better of me if I am a loyal person. I am driven to be with her by the fact that she and I have a growing relationship with each other. It is the pleasure and the power of that relationship that affects not only my conduct toward her, but also the way I live all of my life. It's not that I'm perfect. She could tell you I am not! The bottom line of my attitudes and activities is the fact that I have a highly valued relationship with her.

That is exactly what it is like to be a follower of Christ. It is not the codes or the catechisms. It's Christ. Because I am His and He is mine, I gladly follow, sit at His feet, surrender, and serve.

It is a pleasure—in fact, a privilege—to have been invited by Christ to be His friend and follower. It is this relationship that provides the power to make my life what it should be for Him.

Unless our relationship with Christ is vibrant and growing,
the transforming power of followership will never take hold.
Radical reformation will be too high a risk.

Unless this relationship is vibrant and growing, the transforming power of followership will never take hold. Radical reformation will be too high a risk. When I am far away from Him, replicating His character and conduct will seem like too tough a chore. When, however, He is the central relationship in my life, radical reformation becomes the intriguing adventure of life.

CHAPTER SEVEN

RADICAL REFORMATION

Transforming Conduct and Character

The Armitage Baptist Church, one of the leading evangelical churches in Chicago, is positioned in the heart of one of the city's toughest neighborhoods. On the anniversary of the murder of Dr. David Gunn, a doctor at an abortion clinic in Florida, pro-abortion activists around the country decided to commemorate the moment with what they called a Night of Resistance. The demonstrations planned for the event would make a distinct point for their cause and would also profile Christians as radical and murderous elements in American society.

For some reason the organizers in Chicago chose Armitage Baptist Church as the focus of their demonstration. I was a guest speaker at Armitage on the Sunday night preceding the demonstration, which was planned for Wednesday—the same night as the church's weekly prayer meeting. The church members were concerned. Yet they courageously resolved to proceed with the prayer meeting and, in fact, to use it to focus on the superiority of the cause of Christ.

For years Armitage Baptist Church has sought to reach its culturally diverse community both by drawing people inside its doors and by demonstrating good works through multiple ministries outside. The church has unashamedly, yet compassionately, stood for righteousness against powerful forces such as gay activism, the pro-abortion movement, and gang-driven violence. As the church members prayerfully prepared to confront the demonstration, my heart was inspired as I detected an unusual sense of calm and confidence. This would be a rather unsettling event for any church, let alone one in a troubled and volatile neighborhood such as this.

As I was returning from a trip a couple of weeks later, a headline in an airline copy of *U.S. News & World Report* caught my attention. The banner over a column by John Leo read, AN ANTI-ANTI-ABORTION RALLY. Feeling a mixture of curiosity and apprehension—aware that journalists seldom try to be objective on social issues such as this—I began to read:

> Demonstrators were supposed to bring whistles and other noise makers to drown out church services. The Women's Action Coalition planned to bring its "drum corps." Flyers posted around town to draw a major crowd urged demonstrators to "Dress to shock and/or impress; Come in costume and show your rage.... This was the pro-choice "Night of Resistance" in Chicago. Rallies were taking place around the country last week to mark the anniversary of the murder of abortion doctor David Gunn. The Chicago demonstration was outside Armitage Baptist Church during its regular Wednesday service..."

Now my attention was riveted.

> The sponsors included Queer Nation (an anarchist youth group), Sister Serpents (an underground women's collective), and the National Committee to Free Puerto Rican P.O.W.s and Political Prisoners. A few demonstrators wore patches that said "Feminist Witch" and "Support Vaginal Pride ..." The church was expecting trouble...

Well, I guess so.

In 1992, a dozen members of Queer Nation were invited as guests to the Easter services there. They interrupted the sermon, blew a whistle, and put condoms in the collection plate. Six were arrested.

More recently, car tires have been slashed, cars vandalized, and pro-gay or pro-abortion graffiti sprayed on the church. The night before the rally, the slogan "Choice or Else" was sprayed on the church, and the church reported that rocks were thrown at the glass doors. The most common chant was "Racist, Sexist, Anti-Gays/ Born-Again Bigots, Go Away!"

Leo added,

The "racist" charge is particularly weird: the Armitage congregation is roughly 30 percent black, 30 percent Hispanic, and 40 percent white. The security force on the steps seemed about half Hispanic. The churches in the Logan Square area, a neighborhood mixed by class and race, may be 60 percent Hispanic, 25 percent white, and 15 percent black. For "Born-again bigots," the congregation has made an unusually successful effort to cut across racial lines.

I wanted to stand on my airplane seat, wave the article for everyone to see, and shout Amen and Amen!

While the crowd chanted about racism, a group of young black men showed up wearing long red jackets that said, "S. H. S. Security." They were from a South Side black Baptist church, the Sweet Holy Spirit, and had come to protect their fellow evangelical church.

Somewhat confused, the woman with the bull horn tried to lead the crowd in singing "Little Boxes," a song about suburban conformity popularized by Pete Seger in the 1960s. It was without a doubt the least appropriate song anyone could have sung about this diverse urban congregation. Next, five yellow buses rolled up and a seemingly endless stream of people poured out . . . They were evangelicals from a second South Side church, mostly black families showing up for the service. More than 1,000 people were now in the church . . . The security men had been singing all along, picking fast-paced music that almost matched the volume of the demonstrators. Now, they gave way to a choir of black kids. The demonstrators were done for. The kids were too good and too loud.[1]

In talking to Charles Lyons, the pastor of Armitage Baptist Church, a few weeks later, I thanked him for helping to build a church under Christ's leadership that on that night told a compelling story even a hostile press could not ignore.

Lyons added a P. S. to John Leo's article. He said that for weeks beforehand, organizers of the Night of Resistance had canvassed homes in the community with leaflets, inviting the residents to join in the demonstration. In a neighborhood that is inclined to support both gay and abortion issues, one might have expected a pretty good turnout. But Lyons noted that not one neighbor joined the demonstration. Asked why not, he said that the neighbors have come to know that Armitage Baptist Church cares for them and is concerned about their needs. When the Chicago school system could not open up on time in fall 1995 because of budget problems, the teachers who attended the church volunteered their time and started a temporary alternative school to fill the gap. Their compassionate commitment to the needs of the community built a loyalty in their neighbors' hearts that even the most hostile opponents could not erode.

The people of Armitage Baptist Church demonstrated the transforming power of Jesus Christ—the kind of transformation He desires in each of His followers. He wants those who come to Him to undergo a radical reformation, a process of change that will affect every aspect of our lives. But for many of us, change is not a welcomed concept. Rather, it's downright threatening.[2]

THE NECESSITY OF CHANGE

How many church members does it take to change a light bulb? "Change?! . . . Who said anything about change?!"

I don't know how many times I've heard people say, "Well, that's just me! You'll have to take me like I am." This "what you see is what you get" attitude almost always refers to some personal deficiency that we have decided not to deal with.

As threatening as change may be, consider where we would be if we had refused to learn to walk, talk, or train for a career. Strange, isn't it, that at some point in life we say, "That's it—I'm staying right here!" and we calcify on the spot. Attitudes like this deny the very essence of the death of Christ on our behalf. He saved us to transform us into His likeness (see 2 Cor. 3:18). And you've got to believe that becoming like Him would be a vast improvement.

Yet we are often deceived into thinking that what we have grown accustomed to is best. In a classic moment of intransigence, the governor of New York, Martin Van Buren, wrote to Andrew Jackson the following appeal to maintain the status quo in the face of what he assumed would be radical change:

> To President Jackson:
>
> The canal system of this country is being threatened by the spread of a new form of transportation known as "railroads." The federal government must preserve the canals for the following reasons:
>
> One: If canal boats are supplanted by "railroads," serious unemployment will result. Captains, cooks, drivers, hostlers, repairmen, and lock tenders will be left without means of livelihood, not to mention the numerous farmers now employed in growing hay for the horses.
>
> Two: Canal boats are absolutely essential to the defense of the United States. In the event of the expected trouble with England, the Erie Canal would be the only means by which we could ever move the supplies so vital to waging modern war.
>
> As you may well know, Mr. President, "railroad" carriages are pulled at the enormous speed of 15 miles per hour by "engines" which, in addition to endangering life and limb of passengers, roar and snort their way through the countryside, setting fire to crops, scaring the livestock, and frightening women and children. The Almighty certainly never intended that people should travel at such breakneck speed.
>
> Martin Van Buren
> Governor of New York

Change threatens our present forms and systems of life. Fully devoted followers will have their entire scope of existence exposed to the transformational leadership of Christ. Get ready. Christ as leader will assault our assumptions about money, friends, enemies, ethnic diversity, career, marriage, parenting, philosophy, and the world in general.

We are often deceived into thinking
that what we have grown accustomed to is best.

Remember Paul Hiebert's insightful paradigm that we looked at in chapter 1: Christianity is a unique experience in which followers are moving toward Christ, who is the attracting center of the entirety of life. The convicting application is that some of us, in smug satisfaction with our spiritual status quo, have arrived at a particular place in our Christian experience and have in essence said, "This is good enough; I think I'll stay right here."

Going into orbit around Christ means stifling any further impulse of movement toward Him. Orbital Christians contradict the very essence of what it means to be followers. Fully devoted followers are involved in a passionate pursuit of Christ and are never satisfied with stagnancy or a stalemate. Yet becoming an orbital Christian is alluring because it is more comfortable and less challenging, and besides, we can always take satisfaction in the fact that there are others whose orbits are farther out than ours.

Getting out of orbit is a followership decision. As we make that choice, we must be aware that it will involve change—sometimes radical change—in our comfortable systems of action, reaction, and attitude. But refusing to deorbitize ourselves denies the essence of who we are in Christ. Followership is a call to resume the adventure—regardless.

I have observed over the years that the vast majority of Christians come to a dead stop in followership. We grow to tolerate our sin with excuses like "everyone's got a few weaknesses," or "I've tried but I'll never change," or "life is hard enough without adding this burden." But more damaging is the fact that when we orbitize, we take our eyes off Christ and put them on ourselves and others. This only leads to self-excused pride and a critical, judgmental spirit toward others.

But there are exceptions.

When I was a pastor in Kokomo, Indiana, a seventy-six-year-old man told me, "Pastor, I'm looking forward to growing in Christ under your ministry." What a refreshing difference—seventy-six and still spiraling toward Christ!

Management specialists like to talk about transformational leadership. Warren Bennis states that "Leaders conquer the context."[3] Nothing says it better about Christ's leadership. Christ seeks to radically alter the essence and expression of both the content and the context of our lives. It's not that He just wants to mess around with us. Nor is it that He doesn't love and accept us the way we are—He does. Rather, the whole point of His redemptive mission is not only to defeat the work of Satan in our lives, but also to repair the damage that fallenness has inflicted on us. It's a restoration project. Christ seeks to take us back to our intended glory as the pinnacle of His creation and to show us life the way He meant it to be. He is undaunted in His pursuit of this purpose.

> *Becoming an orbital Christian is alluring*
> *because it is more comfortable and less challenging;*
> *we can always take satisfaction in the fact that there*
> *are others whose orbits are farther out than ours.*

When Christ concluded His call with the admonition "I will make you fishers of men," He was giving fair notice that followers can expect to experience significant change. When we follow Him, nothing is safe from His reforming touch. He is committed to reforming our conduct and our character. Little else matters to Him.

THE UNCONVENTIONAL CHRIST

Marshall Sashkin, adjunct professor at George Washington University, notes that "Followers are transformed because they internalize the values of the organization. The task of the leader is to disseminate the organization's principles and to enunciate the values that animate the organization."[4] Christ's focus in our lives is to lead us to internalize the values of His kingdom and to animate our lives with His ways. His words and ways were radically different from the religious establishment of His day. His popular appeal was most often forged out of the reality that all that He said and did rang true in the hearts of the listeners and watchers. It was as though someone had at last uncovered reality in a world that had been manipulated and managed by principles and practices that, while generally accepted, were nonetheless inadequate and often favored the powerful and highly positioned. Christ's teaching was peppered with life-transitioning phrases such as "You have heard that it was said, . . . but I tell you. . . ."

Nowhere is the radically transforming leadership of Christ more evident than in the Sermon on the Mount. The underlying tenet of the sermon is that all of life must be viewed beyond the boundaries of this present world. Eternity is the benchmark by which every earthly issue is measured.

Christ reversed the assumption that the highly favored and the powerful were the ones who really counted. The meek, the mourners, the poor in spirit were highly honored. He toppled the ever-prevalent notion that externals reflect who and what we really are. He took us beyond action and held His listeners accountable for attitudes and thoughts. He put enemies, money, critical attitudes, and the value of peace and people in paradigms never thought of before. And then, after these unusual and non-mainstream perspectives on life, He likened those who hear and refuse to follow to people who build a house on the sand and leave themselves vulnerable in the day of judgment. By contrast, those who would follow are like a wise person who builds the house of his life on solid rock.

*Christ's actions and reactions in the Gospels
appear equally as radical as His teachings.*

As we follow Christ through the Gospels, His actions and reactions appear equally as radical as His teachings. No one He meets is exempt from His care and compassion, regardless of one's status or position. As shocking as it was to the self-righteous of His day, He mixed with the wealthy and the poor, the tax collector and the prostitute. This was unsettling to those who judgmentally stood at arm's length from these kinds of people. He was never intimidated by the prevailing norms of behavior or the power of the leaders. He spared no room for those who oppress, as became evident in His cleansing of the temple. He was never seduced by the crowd; He pulled no punches in His teaching even if the people were to walk away and never return. He refused to use His miraculous powers to His own gain and glory. He came, refusing to be tempered or tampered with. He knew that His mission was to seek and save the lost, and He worked toward that end regardless of the cost. And ultimately the cost was His own life on an ancient instrument of cruel torture.

When Christ the transformational leader came, He imposed on this fallen world the culture of eternity. He had come from there and would return. He was aware that eternity is the real forever world and that this flat, temporary world is a distorted and deluded one. He never lost His sense of reality, of how life was meant to be.

I am amused at how often we bemoan spending too much time in our "Christian cloisters" and say, "We need to learn how to live in the real world." Wrong! Christ's world is the real world. We need to learn how to live successfully by projecting the real world according to Christ into the fallen world around us. And that requires that we permit Christ to change us to be conformed to His world (Rom. 12:1–2).

Christ made a difference because He was different. For a follower, it is okay to be different. In fact, if we embrace Him and His truth, our character and conduct will make us quite different from the people around us. Those who refuse to follow can ridicule and marginalize us, but in the end followers will be proved right.

Paul Harvey tells the story of a boy who was marginalized because he was different—a boy whose perspectives were profound.

The Rev. Harry Pritchett, Junior, is rector of All Saints Episcopal Church in Atlanta. His church includes specific ministries for the poor, for street people, for college students. It is Dr. Pritchett who called my attention to a boy named Philip.

He was nine—in a Sunday school class of eight-year-olds. Eight-year-olds can be cruel.

The third-graders did not welcome Philip to their group. Not just because he was older. He was "different." He suffered from Down's syndrome and its obvious manifestations: facial characteristics, slow responses, symptoms of retardation.

One Sunday after Easter the Sunday school teacher gathered some of those plastic eggs—the kind in which some ladies' pantyhose are packaged. Plastic eggs which pull apart in the middle.

The Sunday school teacher gave one of these plastic eggs to each child.

On that beautiful spring day each child was to go outdoors and discover for himself some symbol of "new life" and place that symbolic seed or leaf or whatever inside his egg. They would then open their eggs one by one, and each youngster would explain how his find was a symbol of "new life."

So . . .

The youngsters gathered 'round on the appointed day and put their eggs on a table, and the teacher began to open them.

One child had found a flower. All the children "oohed" and "aahed" at the lovely symbol of new life.

In another was a butterfly. "Beautiful," the girls said. And it's not easy for an eight-year-old to say "beautiful."

Another egg was opened to reveal a rock. Some of the children laughed.

"That's crazy!" one said. "How's a rock supposed to be like a 'new life'?"

Immediately a little boy spoke up and said, "That's mine. I knew everybody would get flowers and leaves and butterflies and all that stuff, so I got a rock to be different."

Everyone laughed.

The teacher opened the last one, and there was nothing inside.

"That's not fair," someone said. "That's stupid," said another.

Teacher felt a tug on his shirt. It was Philip. Looking up he said, "It's mine. I did do it. It's empty. I have new life because the tomb is empty."

The class fell silent.

From that day on Philip became part of the group. They welcomed him. Whatever had made him different was never mentioned again.

Philip's family had known he would not live a long life; just too many things wrong with the tiny body. That summer, overcome with infection, Philip died.

On the day of his funeral nine eight-year-old boys and girls confronted the reality of death and marched up to the altar—not with flowers.

Nine children with their Sunday school teacher placed on the casket of their friend their gift of love—*an empty egg.*[5]

For all of us who cringe at the thought of being noticeably different as Christ transforms us, we must remember that those who reject and taunt us for our uniqueness will be among the masses on that day when every knee will bow, affirming at last that Christ's way is the right way to the glory of the Father (Phil. 2:10–11).

CHANGING CONDUCT

The issue, then, is how do we trigger His transforming work in us? This happens in several ways.

We must recognize that He acts on the point of change that is most strategic. Not surprisingly, this will often be the point of our greatest resistance. If we are living by our passions, He will challenge our flirtations and sexual addictions. If we harbor bitterness, He will call us to discard that long-standing grudge that has seemingly protected us, expressed our rage, and satisfied our sense of hurt. If we are addicted to our glory and gain in the workplace, He will require a new perspective that transforms our job from a place of self-serving to a platform for advancing His kingdom. He probes into our homes as to what kind of spouses we will be and how we will manage our parenting.

Christ acts on the point of change that is
most strategic. Not surprisingly, this will often
be the point of our greatest resistance.

As we confront Christ's demands, we will face a strong temptation to go back into orbit. If we adjust our use of sex to glorify Him, we will lose the momentary satisfactions that have become meaningful. What if, in the process of untangling from secret out-of-bounds behavior, someone finds out what we've really been like? What if forgiving means that our offender gets away scot-free? What if we become vulnerable to that person again? What if we have grown to dislike our spouses and have built a system that accommodates that dislike?

The what-ifs are like demons that swoop into our commitment as followers and threaten to choke any capacity to follow this Christ who so compellingly calls.

Can you come to Him in all your vulnerability and insecurity? Can you believe Him when He says, "Come to me, all you who are weary and burdened, and I will give you rest" (Matt. 11:28)? Can you believe that there is no price too high to pay to experience the privilege of walking with Him? Deep within all of us the desire to follow resonates. We really do want life the way it was meant to be, not the way that we have made it. There is only one way to take the risk of letting Him transform our lives, and that is to trust Him. He is worthy and wonderful. What could be good or valuable enough to put between Him and you?

Effective change can only be generated from the impetus of a relationship with Christ. He is the only one worth the unsettling adjustment of tampering with the key components of our lives. He patiently works with us. Followers take all their uncertainty into His companionship and then find in Him the overriding certainty of His steadfast love and wisdom.

Jennifer had lived in the shadow of being abused until she was in her mid-teens. It was her secret. She felt damaged. The memories haunted her and affected not only her self-image, but also her capacity to enjoy intimate relationships. Distancing herself from people was a means of protection. Men, sexuality, closeness, life in general, and even God were seen through the filter of her past.

A friend urged Jennifer to step out of the shadow of her past and get a clear view of Christ. Slowly she became willing to risk this. She knew that it would mean vulnerability, uncertainty, and learning to live life from a radically rearranged perspective. Could she trust her friend, Janet? Would she be able to trust God? Would He abuse her, take advantage of her, and disappoint her?

Janet showed her the real Christ. Jennifer's initial disorientation was like walking from a dark room into the summer sunshine. Though the darkness had become more comfortable, she felt the warmth of Janet's love and knew that it was a reflection of the Christ whom Janet followed. Jennifer began to see more clearly, and it was the real Christ whom she was seeing. She chose to trust Him with her entire life and in time became willing to forgive her offenders—not for their sakes, because they really didn't deserve it, but for Christ's sake. When forced into a choice between forgiving and breaking her relationship with Christ, she readily forgave. The process took time, and the willingness to trust Christ in the midst of her insecurities was a big step. But it was her growing relationship with Christ, along with Janet's help, that provided the energy and impetus to begin to know the freedom to follow and to enjoy life the way it was meant to be.

When Christ wanted to dramatically transform the apostle Paul's life, He appeared to him on the Damascus Road. It was Paul's encounter with Christ that gave the impetus for such a radical and productive change.

When Paul wrote of growing in our walk with Christ, he spoke in terms of fruit. Fruit is the result of a process. We don't manufacture fruit. We do everything else to make it happen—planting, watering, weeding—but the fruit is the effective product of a proven process. The pattern is clear. Paul taught us to "walk in the Spirit" (a New Testament metaphor for following Christ, KJV) so that we would "not gratify the desires of the sinful nature" (Gal. 5:16).

Transformation begins with a fully surrendered, growing, personal relationship with Christ.

John affirms,

This is the message we have heard from him and declare to you: God is light; in him there is no darkness at all. If we claim to have fellowship with him yet walk in the darkness, we lie and do not live by the truth. But if we walk in the light, as he is in the light, we have fellowship with one another, and the blood of Jesus, his Son, purifies us from all sin (1 John 1:5–7).

In 1995 the Chicago area had a dramatic view of an eclipse of the sun. Hours before the total eclipse, the sky and everything it illumined began to turn an eerie gray. The more the sun was eclipsed, the more distorted and dismal the landscape became. The flowers that grace the Moody campus lost their brilliance—a reminder that it is a clear loss to be out of the clear view of the sun for even a short while. If we sense that life is drab, haunting, unsettling, and dismal, then perhaps we should check what is eclipsing the Son.

> *If we sense that life is drab, haunting,*
> *unsettling, and dismal, then perhaps we*
> *should check what is eclipsing the Son.*

I suppose we could become accustomed to life in the darkness. We may even come to like how things are working out in the shade. Our careers may be on track, that affair may be filling a huge void, self-centeredness may be protective and handy as we seek to cut our own wake. But those periodic glances to the edge of our shadowed existence keep haunting us, compelling us to move forward. At times we have even seen the Son welcoming us to His new and transforming way. He will not join us in the shadows. He can't. But He is there in the light, waiting. He waits to transition our lives from normal, well-worn thoroughfares of action and attitude to walk in His unique, intriguing ways.

TREADING NEW PATHS

Witt Stephens, as investment banker from Arkansas, tells the story of a trail made by a calf three hundred years ago. He describes how the trail turned into a path as dogs and sheep walked in the calf's footsteps. Behind them were people who, while complaining about the winding path, walked it anyway. The path became a lane, then a road, then a village street, then a thoroughfare. Stephens writes,

So people two centuries and a half
Trod the footsteps of that calf.
A hundred thousand people were led
By one calf three centuries dead
For we are prone to go it blind
Along the calf paths of our mind
And work from sun to sun
To do what other people have done.[6]

Christ as our leader takes us from the jeopardy of the twisted, mindless calf paths of our day and calls to His straight, though sometimes narrow, way. The word for *following* in Matthew 4:20 that depicts the disciples' response not only denotes a relationship but also comes from the root word that means "path."[7] This root lent meaning to the sense that a follower in the time of Christ was one who was found "in the way" with a person. This word picture offers a profound image of Christ's transformational leadership. He came into our world with its well-worn paths of conventional wisdom and traditional habits; He refused to walk the paths cut by basic instincts, cultural attitudes, philosophical musings about life and liberty, religionist codes for behavior, and other socially acceptable patterns of life. He arrived on our turf and announced, "I am the Way," and proceeded to take the machete of divine wisdom and cut through the underbrush of our fallenness, forging fresh, new paths. He walks these paths ahead of us and looks back over His shoulder to see if anyone is in the way with Him.

In a world that celebrates paths of self-protection through anger and revenge, Waymaker Jesus has cut a path of meekness, forgiveness, and love. He walked it all the way to the Cross. Followers are found on this road with Him.

No aspect of our lives is exempt from Christ's new and correct way. He leaves nothing untouched. Relationships, time, money, self, children, career, talents, focus of life, and anything else that gets caught up in the traffic of life are radically rerouted when we follow Him.

The path that Christ cut lies in a clear direction. He is taking us somewhere: to heaven. Everything He did and taught has eternity in view. Most of us give a nod of our theology to heaven and then live as though this world is all we have. The greatest trap of a wanna-be follower is the trap of temporalism. If life is not defined by the long view, if all we have is the here and now, then we are vulnerable to materialism, hedonism, sensualism, the pursuit of prosperity, power, and position at all costs—and the disappointment and despair that inevitably result.

> *Everything Christ did and taught has eternity*
> *in view. Most of us give a nod of our theology to heaven*
> *and then live as though this world is all we have.*

Peggy Noonan, former speech writer for Presidents Bush and Reagan, was dead right when she wrote in *Forbes* magazine,

> I think we have lost the old knowledge that happiness is over-rated—that, in a way, life is overrated. We have lost, somehow, a sense of mystery—about us, our purpose, our meaning, our role. Our ancestors believed in two worlds, and understood this to be the solitary, poor, nasty, brutish and short one. We are the first generations of man that actually expected to find happiness here on earth, and our search for it has caused such—unhappiness. The reason: If you do not believe in another, higher world, if you believe only in the flat material world around you, if you believe that this is your only chance at happiness—if that is what you believe, then you are not disappointed when the world does not give you a good measure of its riches, you are despairing.[8]

C. S. Lewis notes, "Aim at heaven and you get earth thrown in. Aim at earth and you get neither."[9]

Eternity is the only reality that can resolve life's insolvable dilemmas. Only an eternal perspective enables us to adequately cope with life's disappointments and frequent downsides. Followers view all of life—its good times as well as its bad—through the lens of eternity. The worth and value of every activity and involvement is ultimately measured not by the bang it creates on this side, but rather by the benefit it contributes to our eternal home. Followers have the marks of eternity clearly evident on every endeavor.

Most of us find that we walk on earth to the sound of many drummers. Our own desires and the desires of those we admire, those who have control over us, or those we are intimidated by are often the impetus for our choices and behavior. Our greed, self-centered agendas, and fear of losing friends, money, or power become the controlling factors for life.

Christ forged a new and far less complex road for us to walk, and He expressed it in two ways—like parallel lanes of a highway. The first was His singular allegiance to His Father in heaven. He often said that He had come to do the Father's will (see, for example, John 4:34; 6:39). The ultimate moment of this lifeway was His agonizing experience in Gethsemane, when He yielded Himself to His Father's will regarding the brutal and lonely experience of the Cross. Followers can reduce all of life to the question, "What is it that my Father in heaven wants for my life in this moment?" Yielding to His will puts us in the way with Christ.

The second was Christ's desire to do everything to the glory of the Father (see, for example, John 8:49–50; 14:13). If we have been forgiving, compassionate, brave in the pursuit of justice, and vocal about oppression and the poor, we cannot in good conscience take the credit when we are applauded. Tactfully giving God the credit is a delight for the fully devoted follower. Moreover, it offers a way to bear witness to the Lord who is the reason why our lifeways have so dramatically changed. Taking the credit ourselves should cause us to examine our motives for serving Christ.

REPLICATING HIS CHARACTER

When I was in seminary, I could almost always tell what a fellow student's major was by listening to him talk or watching his gestures and teaching mannerisms. He had become so enthralled with his major professor that he used words, phrases, and styles of thinking and speaking that were mirror images of his admired mentor.

Another nuance to the word used in Matthew 4:20 to describe the disciples' commitment indicates that those who would be known as followers were so impressed by their leader that they often ended up replicating His traits in their lives. This issue is deeper than conduct.

It relates to character. Therefore, when the Epistles speak of followership, they usually use the word *imitate*. Followers of Christ are clearly enamored with Him, and thus their lives emulate Him. The expanding character of Christ in my life becomes by far the most important element in my existence as a follower. Unlike the travelers on the crowded byways of my world that celebrate competency and credentials, a follower of Christ is known by his character. That character, when people see it clearly enough, is a compelling reflection of Christ as our Leader.

> *The issue of commitment is deeper*
> *than conduct. It relates to character.*

Christ's power lay neither in competency as our world sees it nor in the kind of credentials that would give Him rank and privilege among the elite. His competency, in earthly terms, extended to His simple skills as a carpenter; His lack of credentials placed Him as an outsider both politically and religiously. Yet He impacted this planet more than any other man before or since. His character was intriguing and compelling. It is His character expressed through our conduct that empowers us to have an incredible impact as fully devoted followers of Him.

The early followers imitated Christ so powerfully that the watching world gave them a nickname. Nicknames are tags given to reflect some unique quality or idiosyncrasy in someone's persona. Elementary school children are particularly brutal about finding some malformation and tattooing it on their friends via a nickname. Mine was "Liver Lips." (Anything that is psychologically wrong with me today is directly attributable to that early childhood scar!) The followers of Christ got nicknamed "Christians." Their detractors noticed that followers are imitators, that they are like Christ.

Character not only marks the life of a follower but also becomes a blessing to others. Think of life with a follower whose character is marked by Christlike qualities such as these:

Integrity measures all the activities of life by the standard of truth. When Christ claimed to be the way and the truth, He meant that He would embody truth in all that He did and was. Integrity is far more than telling the truth. It means living a life that is consistent with the truth whether in public or in private. Its opposites are hypocrisy and duplicity.

Humility is not a quiet, reserved, super-sanctimonious posture in life. The truly humble person can be appropriately bold and can enjoy life to the fullest—laughing and crying with great expression. Humility is the driving desire to give God the glory in all things and to obey Him regardless. Humility can mark great leadership. Christ was authentically humble, as was Moses. The counterpart to humility—pride—seeks to take glory to itself and to seize control at strategic crossroads. "God opposes the proud but gives grace to the humble" (1 Peter 5:5).

Compassion is the ability to get beyond the press of our own interests and respond to the needs of others. It is more than a feeling; it is active in amassing resources to bring comfort and solution. Compassion listens, contemplates life from another's point of view, knows no barriers of color or culture, and clearly seeks to bless rather than be blessed. A lack of compassion produces quick, judgmental responses and uninterested withdrawal from others in need.

Purity is the quality in our lives that cancels wrong motives and insincerity and produces a person who is trustworthy and exemplary. Purity denotes conformity to righteousness and expresses itself in every arena of life. Our view of, and involvement with, people, money, things, sex, opportunities, thoughts, and time can all be characterized by a reflection of that which is truly good and right. Purity is an aspect of God's holiness and is increasingly reflected by loyal followers of Christ.

Generosity is the flip side of greed. Followers are generous with all their resources within the priorities that honor Christ. Followers are generous with the cause of the kingdom. They are generous with their family, then their friends, then fellow followers, and ultimately with all who pass their way. Generosity involves time, talents, money, possessions, and anything else within the sphere of our control.

Contentment accepts what God has provided with a thankful spirit, enabling us to pursue righteousness rather than a long list of coveted things. We are to be content with our money, our spouses, our material possessions, our gifts, and our lot in life.

In addition to these qualities, followers reflect Christ's tolerance for the sinner, courage, faith, and self-sacrifice.

Character has a distinct advantage over credentials and competency. Character leaves a legacy; competency makes a living. Character is transferable to succeeding generations; credentials are buried with us. Character makes others believe that they can also achieve a life marked by character. Character excites others to growth; credentials and competency discourage others and cause tension and division. Character is attainable by all; credentials and competency are available to only a few.

How would you know a follower of Christ if you saw one? He or she would bear a resemblance to Christ in both conduct and character.

Followers reform their lives in these two important areas. To transition toward effective change, followers should—

- Make a short list of the areas of both conduct and character in which you would like to grow. Review the list with a friend who knows you well. He or she is most able to help you prioritize the most strategic endeavors.

- Focus on these areas as the pursuit of your life. Paul exhorted Timothy, "But you, man of God, flee from all this, and pursue righteousness, godliness, faith, love, endurance and gentleness" (1 Tim. 6:11).

- Pray these items back to God, repenting when necessary and pleading for God's work in your life to grow in these areas.

- Seek forgiveness from those who have been hurt in the past by your conduct and character faults.

- Study and memorize Scripture, particularly the passages where the issues on your list are most clearly addressed.

- Find additional friends to whom you can be accountable for growth in these areas.

- Be around people who reflect more of His character and conduct so that you can find motivation and hope to grow as they have.
- Realize that growth takes time and is best cultivated in the ground of a growing intimacy with Christ.

Christ rescues us from a life headed the wrong way. When we are found in His way, our lives become radically different.

One of the decisive battles of World War II was won by a clever and simple scheme. As a large brigade of Germany advanced, a small group of Allied forces was sent to divert its way. As the German army approached a crossroads, the sign that pointed toward their destination turned them across a bridge that spanned a wide river. The group of Allies poised themselves with explosives to detonate the bridge as the Germans passed over. The bridge exploded, killing many of the Germans and stranding the rest on the other side. The Germans' problem was that they were headed in the wrong direction. The allies had turned the signposts away from the correct road and pointed them across the bridge. Unknowingly, the Germans were on the wrong road, and the consequences were devastating.

Christ rescues us from a life headed the wrong way. He welcomes followers to His way, and fully devoted followers are found in the way with Him. When we are found in His way, our lives become radically different.

CHAPTER EIGHT

THE COMPELLING CAUSE

Where Will He Take Us?

It was a day like most days in the office for me—full of appointments, meetings, paperwork, and correspondence. That is, it was routine until 3:40, when someone burst through the door with a flushed face, announcing that a gunman was holding staff and students hostage in our athletic center and had threatened to kill someone if his demands weren't met. I grabbed my coat and ran for the door, and as I made my way across the campus I could see police cars and news vans.

The campus of the Moody Bible Institute is efficiently secured against this kind of danger, but it became apparent to me that no one or no place is ultimately safe from those who seek to do harm. I found myself standing on the sidewalk outside the building, waiting and wondering if I would soon hear a shot that would signal the beginning of great measures of grief and sorrow to all of us on the campus and loved ones in far-off places.

We learned that about twenty-five students were seated on the floor of the lobby, a faculty member was being held as a human shield, two staff members were on either side of the man, and members of Chicago's police force who had hostage-crisis training were poised behind pillars in the lobby with their guns aimed directly at the per-petrator of the crime, who claimed to have a gun.

I stood traumatized on the sidewalk, processing all the possibilities that might grow out of this crisis in the minutes that stretched ahead of us. It was a disruption that was more than unwelcome. I wanted to resist it with everything within me. Yet I knew that above and beyond it, there was a powerful God whose sovereign oversight of our lives includes even disruptions as devastating as this.

As we waited, students began to be released one by one, then the staff, and then the faculty member who was held as a human shield. Needless to say, we breathed a deep and grateful sigh of relief. Then I saw the police force lead this man in handcuffs to the police wagon.

The details of what had happened began to unfold for us. This man had walked up to the information desk and demanded that a local television station be brought in so he could air his complaints before all of Chicago. He said he was armed—police discovered he actually was not—and if his demands were not met, he would shoot anyone in sight. As he took hostages among the staff and a class that was just dismissing, he held them in the face of the police force who stood at rifle's length away in the lobby.

In the midst of this, one student seated on the floor raised his hand to get the man's attention and asked if he might pray with him. The man looked startled and said, "That would be good. I need your prayers." The student prayed. Then another prayed, and then anoth-er. Then the man began releasing the individual students as they prayed.

Meanwhile, the faculty member and one of the staff members explained to the man that God really loved him and that although he had come to the campus meaning to do harm, God had really brought him there to hear the good news that Jesus Christ cared for him and could not only save his life but also help him in his present circumstances. The staff member led the man through the whole plan of salvation step by step.

This was turning out to be one of the most unique evangelistic endeavors ever to take place on our campus. Apparently at gunpoint and in the midst of what would normally be devastating trauma, courageous and confident people were getting beyond their own distress to care compassionately for the soul of one who had put their lives at risk. I am confident that the police officers, who had been involved in many similar situations, had never experienced anything quite like this before. I think even today of the witness in the hearts of these policemen as they saw a dramatically different response to one of life's most challenging moments.

That night I sat in my living room and watched the news as the major channels in Chicago reported on this event. Over and over again, I heard the reporters say that "the students at Moody Bible Institute prayed for this one who had taken them hostage." What a resounding affirmation of the unique difference that Jesus Christ makes in our lives before a watching world!

> *The events at the Institute underscored the reality*
> *that God has called us not to safety but to service.*

God obviously had permitted this event, despite the well-planned campus security, to enable us to reach out to someone in desperate need. Students continue to work with this man while he sits in jail.

In the Moody chapel service the day after the hostage crisis, we took the opportunity to put this in biblical perspective, emphasizing the fact that even though we may take every possible measure to be safe and secure, there are no safe places in this world. Further, we underscored the reality that God has called us not to safety but to service. Moreover, many of God's finest people throughout history have been willing to serve others for the sake of Christ in the face of great danger. This was clearly a teaching and training moment for the students that called them to renew their confidence, courage, and commitment to follow Christ in the midst of deep crisis.

These students knew that followers focus on people and eternal needs regardless of the consequences.

THE PRIORITY OF PEOPLE

Compelling causes marshal great followings. World War II was launched because of the threat of the tyrant Hitler. The European conflict hardly seemed much of our business until Pearl Harbor erupted in a rain of Japanese bombs. At that point it was not difficult to draft enlistees in the cause. The entire nation rallied to the moment. Sons and daughters put themselves willingly in harm's way. Factories changed their venues to accommodate the needs of war. America became preoccupied with the cause.

The conflict in Vietnam was a different story. To many, the struggle to preserve the sovereignty of South Vietnam was not a cause worthy of the price. While many valiant patriots sacrificed themselves for the cause, its validity eluded many others.

If Christ says, "Follow Me," then it is valid to inquire where He will take us.

And the answer is clear: "I will make you fishers of men" (Matt. 4:19).

Jesus Christ is, and was, passionately addicted to people. Having come from eternity past, and given that He was on His way to eternity future, Christ was well aware that the only entity of true value and worth on this earth is people. They are the only eternal commodities; everything else will be held at the border. So it is no wonder that Jesus was consumed with people, their relationship to Him, and their eternal destiny. And if that is where He is headed, then that is where followers will be found as well. Authentic followers focus the attention of their lives and resources on the spiritual potential and eternal destiny of mankind. Is there a greater cause?

Christ was well aware that the only entity
of true value and worth on this earth is people.

When it comes to following, Christ wants to control the outcomes, and He has determined that the only outcome of any value is the enhancement and advancement of others in the light of their eternal needs and relationship to Him.

Two friends of mine, Jerry and Dee Miller, followed Christ away from a lucrative career with a major oil company to serve a Christian organization. This organization had a vision to launch a conference center in the North Carolina mountains to train Christians in the Word and work of Christ. While Christ obviously doesn't call all of us to give up our careers, that is what He had in mind for Jerry and Dee when He said, "Follow Me."

Jerry was just a few years away from retirement. When he inquired about taking an early retirement, the company told him that they couldn't afford to lose him and wouldn't grant him his request. Following Christ into this Christian organization now meant that Jerry and Dee would have to leave their pension and retirement benefits behind and start all over again. The choice for them was the cause or their career. They chose the cause.

For the Millers, following became a matter of letting go of much that is temporal to participate with Christ in all that is eternal. Today Jerry and Dee have the privilege of seeing thousands being exposed to the life-changing truths of God's Word. The impact of their decision is multiplied on a macro scale as believers return to their own homes and communities and reproduce and replicate the work of Christ through their lives.

Howard Dahl received a different call. Howard launched a farm implement company and groomed it into an enterprise that saw its impact spread to international markets. Because of the company's success, Howard was approached by two of the nation's largest farm implement companies about acquiring the business.

But that is not the most important part of Howard's story. If that's all there were, it would be just another story about nothing more than money, pride, and bragging rights.

Rather, Howard built his business as a follower of Christ. The driving force of his vision was not first and foremost the building of a personal empire or the pleasure of its economic benefits. It was to build a business that reflected the reality of Christ's character in terms of the people it touched. For Howard, the measure of his success was not primarily the bottom line, but whether or not the difference that Christ makes was evident to others. And the difference was evident. Being a fully devoted follower affected the way he treated his employees, the quality of his product, the type of service he offered, the company's marketing strategies, and the attitude he held toward even his fiercest competitors. Being a follower of Christ even impacted the way he distributed his profits. For Howard, the end result of his business was not the implements that were loaded from his dock; it was that the production of these implements would draw others to Christ.

Howard's career was not his calling. It was where he fulfilled his calling as a follower.

He had not only been impacted by the compelling nature of Christ in terms of conduct and character, but also understood that to be a fully devoted follower meant to be fully focused on the cause.

Granted, most of us cannot manage the companies we work for so that they reflect the character of Christ and draw others to Him. For us, the cause means that we do our work as followers in ways that reflect Christ and express the distinct difference that Christ can make in a life. Followers who embrace the cause see everything that is under their control as an instrument to impact their world. Parents see their homes as places where love, peace, forgiveness, nurturing grace, and protective power are displayed. Following parents see their primary role not as controlling their kids—although that is a parental responsibility—but as communicating the reality of Christ to their children. Following means that we don't see our children as extensions of our pride and dreams but as real persons who also can become followers of Christ and impact their world for Him—whether they become doctors, lawyers, butchers, bakers, candlestick makers, pastors, or missionaries.

The liberating reality of all of this is that nothing in life is more important than Christ and His cause. All of life's decisions and attitudes are formed by this dynamic. Everything of value in our treasure chest—whether it be money, career, friends, possessions, or property—is all there for the cause. Everything within our grasp is a means to reflect the compelling Christ to those who need Him.

The early disciples not only saw Christ as a compelling person worthy of their full devotion but also heard Him call them to a compelling cause. Which would it be: a life consumed with piles of fish or a life that touches people with the transforming, liberating work and worth of Christ? It is hardly a decision, given that the choice involves the human dilemma of separation from Christ and the jeopardy of our eternal destiny. The cause is about getting beyond the fish, beyond all that is temporal. It is about seeing everything in our lives as platforms from which Christ can be seen and heaven placed in view.

The cause is carried out against society's preoccupation with our own needs rather than the needs of others. Just as the idea of following flies in the face of a culture bent on autonomy and self-governance, so the thought of committing one's life to becoming a "fisher of men" runs counter to a society addicted to self-centeredness. Following, at the very essence of its expression, is an other-directed endeavor.

Our commitment to follow Christ does not bestow instant perfection. Moving from the call to the cause takes time.

It is clear from even a casual reading of Scripture that the disciples struggled with self-focused perspectives even after committing themselves to following Christ. Followership begins with a commitment to Christ as the undisputed, unconditional leader. This commitment, however, does not bestow instant perfection. Moving from the call to the cause takes time. The transition is measured by how effective my "otherness" is now as compared with how it was two, three, or six months ago. The question is, "Is my commitment to the spiritual needs and eternal destinies of others closer to Christ's responses now than it has been in the past?" Or, "Does life still revolve around me and my concerns?"

When it comes to the cause, we are often seen following at a distance. Christ is always seeking to shrink the distance between Himself and His fully devoted followers. He loves it when we get close.

GETTING CLOSE

Remember those early days of romance—when you would walk up the sidewalk, knock on the door, and pick up your date? As you walk her to the car, you're wondering if she likes you as much as she said she did. The test of her interest is soon to come. You open the car door for her, and as you walk around to the driver's side you are hoping that she has slid across the seat to sit as close to you as possible (one of the few benefits of not having seat belts or bucket seats). If she was hugging the other door, it was not a good sign—especially if she said, "You ought to be happy that at least I'm in your car."

What a devastating way to start the evening!

I wonder whether that's how Christ perceives us. He courted us, knocked on the door of our hearts, placed us into a redemptive relationship, and asked us to follow Him. Yet often He finds us following afar off. He has created us for intimacy with Him, and He anticipates that we will seek that intimacy by immersing outselves ever more deeply in the cause. He loves it when we get close and works patiently yet surely to shrink the distance.

When it came to embracing the cause, there were at least three situations in which the distance between the disciples and Christ was huge: The first concerned the ongoing struggle to establish a position of power and influence in relationships with others; the second, the propensity to be discompassionate to the needs of others; and the last, the instinctive, natural barriers to understanding that exist between Christ-followers and the lost. Each of these settings created among the disciples a dramatic picture of our own struggle to embrace the cause. Yet, as difficult as these are, to be a fully devoted follower means that we are making marked progress in the areas of servanthood, sensitivity, and seeing.

DESCENDING INTO GREATNESS

It has always been fascinating to me that Jesus' disciples, who were the consummate followers, had such a hard time getting close to their leader in regard to their own perceived importance. Time and again, the Gospels relate their running debate about which of them would be the greatest in the kingdom. Like contestants in a beauty contest or athletes on the eve of the professional draft, the disciples anxiously waited to see whether they would be selected for the most important posts in the kingdom that they believed Christ would establish on the earth in the near future. So pervasive was this impulse that even on the night before the Crucifixion they were discussing this topic in the Upper Room, which prompted Christ to graphically demonstrate the distance by dropping His robe and putting a towel around His waist to wash their feet as a servant.

It is striking just when this urge for place, power, and prestige became painfully apparent. During Christ's final trek to Jerusalem, James and John approached Christ with their mother, who asked on their behalf if they can be the ones to sit by Him—one on His right hand, the other on the left (Matt. 20:20–28). We can understand why a mother might wonder about the future of her sons. With a mother's keen insight, she might have asked her sons whether Christ understood how capable they were and how blessed the kingdom would be if they were given leadership roles. And her sons no doubt would have said, "We can't say that to Him," leaving the door wide open to her proposing, "Then I'll go and ask for you"—to which neither of the men objected, since they went with her to file the petition.

The rest of the disciples became furious when they heard the news. Not only had they been beaten to the punch, but they had been outmaneuvered through a sneaky trick—namely, James and John using their mother to gain advantage. The distress and division were so evident that Christ moved in to rescue the situation and again patiently worked to reduce the distance.

Robert was a senior executive in a high-profile business in his community. His leadership and management skills were well known. Being committed to Christ, he and his wife, Molly, had a deeply held commitment to their local church. Robert had always felt that if he were ever to be chosen an elder, he would be a good one. He secretly wished that he could serve in this way. Elections were coming up again, and his name was being considered. What troubled him, however, was that a relatively new church member appeared to be lobbying for a place on the ballot. This new member had taken the pastor out to lunch and had entertained the chairman of the nominating committee to eighteen holes of golf at the local country club. On several different occasions Robert had heard the man telling others about the influential positions he had held in his former church.

Robert confided his sense of frustration to his best friend, Barry. Barry pointed out that Christ was looking for servants, not leaders, and showed him Matthew 20:20–28. "The issue in terms of the cause of Christ," Barry said, "is not the position you hold in the work of Christ but whether or not what you do with your life draws others to Him."

This was a whole new way of thinking to Robert. If in God's providence he was not selected for eldership, he thought of a number of ways he could serve Christ to attract others to Him. He had been asked earlier in the year to serve as an usher. He was ashamed to recognize that he thought the role was beneath his dignity. Now he realized that it might make a profound impact if friends and acquaintances who knew of his status in the community were to see him ushering for his Christ. Another way to serve, he realized, was to take a colleague or even a competitor to lunch—time better spent than seeking to advance himself by courting the power players at church.

Robert's new orientation to the cause reflected the words of Christ to His position-hungry disciples: "You know that the rulers of the Gentiles lord it over them, and their high officials exercise authority over them. Not so with you. Instead, whoever wants to become great among you must be your servant, and whoever wants to be first must be your slave" (Matt. 20:25–27). Then Christ used Himself as the example. Pointing out that they obviously didn't understand that in the kingdom it was the servants who were great, He said, "The Son of Man did not come to be served, but to serve, and to give his life as a ransom for many" (v. 28).

We must never take for granted the reality
that when the God of the universe became a man,
He chose to come in the form of a servant.

Unfortunately, much of the energy of Christ's cause has been sucked into our own self-centered agendas. Rarely do people come into a church family seeking to serve; more often, they have a consumer's mind-set: What will this church do for me? Will it meet my needs, hold my interest, thrill my soul, solve my loneliness? We even tend to view our nonchurch involvements in community and the lives of others in terms of personal advantage.

The cause of Christ is empowered by fully devoted followers who get close to Him by seeing themselves as servants to others for the cause of eternity. We must never take for granted the reality that when the God of the universe became a man, He chose to come in the form of a servant (Phil. 2:5–11). It is a staggering thought that out of all the attributes He could have chosen, He chose humility so as to empower us toward growth and glory.

WHO CARES?

The disciples who first followed Christ were dreadfully out of step with His cause when they pointed out a blind beggar and asked Christ who had sinned—the man's parents, or he in his mother's womb—that he should be born blind (John 9:1–7). No doubt they had seen this beggar many times before and had reacted with the same kind of theological curiosity. What they saw in Christ's response was hardly stand-offish. It clearly demonstrated the distance between Christ and His followers in regard to responding to people's needs. His was a response of compassion, not curiosity and judgment. He marshaled His resources to grant sight to the beggar and claimed that the blindness was actually intended to provide a moment when God could be magnified through Christ's compassionate touch.

Aren't we just like those detached disciples? When we hear of trouble in someone's life we are far more interested in the details and an analysis of what, why, when, and where than we are in finding out what we can do to reach out and help.

It is amazing what a note, a listening ear, a season of prayer, a hug (with no lecture about the sovereignty of God), a meal, or some free baby-sitting with the children can mean. I have had the pleasure of pastoring churches that were full of followers who went beyond the curiosity to the compassion. What I found interesting was that unsaved relatives and friends were consistently impressed with the uniqueness of a caring community. No doubt they wondered, if similar fates were to befall them, who would rally to their support? If we would only learn to see tragedy as a platform to demonstrate the power of God's glory through us, we could have a far greater impact on our world than we do. Anyone can be curious. Followers are compassionate.

We can't miss the note of judgment that lodged in the disciples' curiosity. "Who sinned?" was the common question asked by those who passed by. "Nobody!" was Christ's astounding answer. We so often appear to be in a search-and-destroy mode while our Leader has a far different perspective. Imagine how the blind beggar felt every time he heard people speculating about the sin that caused his blindness. It was bad enough to be blind.

Anyone can be curious. Followers are compassionate.

Then imagine the refreshing, compelling contrast he must have felt when Someone came by and said that he would be an opportunity to display the glory of God—and then felt the healing power of Christ's compassionate touch. How powerfully unique!

When is the last time we took the opportunity to start acting on our beliefs, not with judgment but with understanding and grace? Followers do it Christ's way.

Few people are more prone to take discompassionate, judgmental views of others than those of us who call ourselves followers. Not unlike the religious folk of Christ's day who felt they had a corner on truth and righteousness, we, too, tend to disenfranchise ourselves and view others through a less-than-caring point of view. From the homeless to the criminal class to others facing social needs, we too often impose an attitude like "why don't they get a job" or "that's what you get when you live that kind of life." It is a kind of biblical version of "you made your bed, now lie in it." Our worst moments consist of our response to those who are engineering America's pagan social agenda. We should never shrink from holding our culture accountable for righteousness, nor from speaking the truth in the face of the rejection of moral standards. But when our anger, rhetoric, and political practices contradict the spirit and standards of Christ and overwhelm our sense of compassion for the lostness of the perpetrators of social deprivations, we no longer display the uniqueness that a follower is intended to express.

Getting close means learning to care and then being willing to do something about it—not for our own glory or gain, but for the glory of our Leader. Without Him we would never have known what it means to get beyond our curiosity or even our crises to take compassionate action.

A DIFFERENT POINT OF VIEW

Another demonstration of how easy it is for fully devoted followers to follow at a distance unfolds in John 4, the story of Christ's encounter with the woman at the well. The account reveals much about how we see people.

In airports and other public places, I often have time on my hands for engaging in one of my favorite indoor sports: people watching. As I watch people walk by, I find myself wondering, where do they come from, where are they going, what do they do for a living, or could they have possibly looked in the mirror this morning?

Christ saw things in people that the disciples failed to see because of their preoccupation with their preferences, prejudices, and—yes—their picnics. What He saw stimulated a totally different response from that of the followers. John 4 discloses that, having sent the disciples into Sychar to bring Him some food, Christ sat by the well, weary from His journey. A woman came to the well, and Christ asked her for a drink. We realize later on that He had a purpose in His request: to introduce the woman to "the water of life."

If I feel weary after a busy day of travel and interaction with people, perhaps the last thing I want to do is to get into a deep conversation with strangers. Yet Christ saw something in this woman that took Him beyond His preferences.

What was it that He saw?

Christ was a rabbi. Rabbis viewed women as less than significant and sources of temptation and potential contamination. No rabbi worth his Torah would be caught dead talking to a woman, especially if they were the only people present. In fact, rabbinical literature indicates that if a rabbi were walking down a street and saw a woman approaching, he would most probably cross to the other side of the street until she passed. Christ saw something in this woman that took Him beyond the prejudices associated with His perceived position as a religious leader.

What was it that He saw?

Not only did Christ see something that took Him beyond personal preference and conventional prejudice, but He also penetrated a cultural barrier because she was a woman of Samaria. The Jews and the Samaritans lived in deep racial polarization. This racial divide related to nearly every aspect of their existence. For centuries the animosity had been thick between them. They had invaded each other's territory, ransacked each other's temples, and generally expressed their disdain in every possible way. It was probably an unsettling thought to His followers that Christ insisted that they go home through Samaria. Yet Christ saw something in the woman that melted the racial-cultural prejudice that usually would have created an inseparable barrier between them.

> *Christ saw things that the disciples failed to see*
> *because of their preoccupation with their preferences,*
> *prejudices, and—yes—their picnics.*

What was it that He saw?

If you add to the equation the fact that He also knew that she was an immoral woman, then you begin to understand what a remarkable interaction this was.

As the story unfolds, Christ whets her appetite for the reality that He is the One that she has been thirsting for. In a climactic moment, He says to her, "I am He whom you seek." She runs back into the city to tell all her friends that she has found the one whom she thinks is indeed the Messiah.

At this point, John reintroduces the disciples into the story. They present themselves in startling contrast to the One they have committed themselves to follow. They marvel that Christ had been talking with a woman. In fact, the account suggests that they are not happily amazed that He is breaking through conventional barriers to speak to this woman's needs. They respond more with consternation than enthusiasm. Yet, according to the account, they say nothing to the Messiah. It is as though they may be muttering under their breath,

"Lord, you're going to wreck everything. There are people in Sychar related to people who live in Jerusalem—what if they hear about this back home!"

Avoiding a sense of confrontation, however, the disciples tell Christ that they have brought His lunch. He responds, "I have food to eat that you know nothing about."

What was it that He saw? Christ saw something so compelling that it eclipsed His appetite.

The disciples wondered if someone had brought Him food. They didn't have a clue as to what was really happening. The distance was huge. Christ was speaking of His preoccupation with His Father's will, and they were concerned with their picnic. The disciples didn't see the woman as Christ saw her.

I am reminded of the new computer-generated art in which at first glance all we can see is a mass of squiggly lines punctuated periodically with small figures. I am told that if we gaze at the picture long enough, the random lines will pull together in our minds to reveal, for example, a scene with palm trees on the beach and porpoises in the bay.

My wife can perceive the picture in a flash. By contrast, I can stand there with a blank stare on my face, looking like an abject fool. In the same way, we too often fail to see people in ways that take us beyond our own preferences, prejudices, and picnics. Like the disciples, we are culturally and materialistically bound up in our own mind-sets.

Christ worked patiently with the disciples to shrink the distance. He called them to lift up their eyes and gaze at the harvest. As He put it, "Look at the fields!" He was not speaking of the wheatfields, but drawing attention to the streams of white robed people who were, by this time, streaming out of Sychar to meet this One who, as the woman put it, "told me everything I ever did."

What did Christ see when He saw the woman? He saw the harvest. She could be—would be—reaped for eternity. When He saw that, His perspective took Him beyond His preferences and prejudices. When He told the disciples that they had to go home through Samaria, He may have done so not only for the Samaritans' sake but for the good of the followers as well—followers who need to look at people and see the harvest.

What do you see when you see people? Fully devoted followers train their perspective to see the harvest and reach out with compassion in intentional and creative ways to serve the cause of eternity. When we are committed to following, Christ will take us places we have never been before and will teach us to see people as we have never seen them before.

> *When we are committed to following, Christ will take us places we have never been before and will teach us to see people as we have never seen them before.*

Following is all about seeing our neighbors as the harvest—that neighbor who mows his grass at 7:30 on Saturday morning or plays heavy metal rock at megadecimals in the apartment above us. It is about seeing the boss not as means of advancement, perks, or pay raises, but rather as one who might be drawn to Christ by seeing the reality of Christ in us. It is about the masses in the stadium and the person in the express checkout who has thirteen items instead of the mandated ten. The harvest is composed of people who are not like us—not from where we are from and not going where we are going.

The verdict in the O. J. Simpson murder trial brought responses that polarized Americans across racial, political, and gender lines. Many of us were caught up in the guessing game. We expressed antipathy for the avowed racist Mark Furman, ambivalence toward Simpson, repulsion for the abuse of his former wife, empathy and regret for Nicole's and Ronald Goodman's families. But who of us thought to pray for O. J.? When did we pray to the Lord that someone would reach Furman with the gospel before it was too late? Or who of us followers cared for Johnnie Cochran's or Marcia Clark's soul? When we saw the wide array of people in the case, what did we see?

Mickey Mantle was my boyhood hero. Growing up not far from the Bronx where "the Mick" played for the New York Yankees, I reveled in every opportunity to see him perform. I batted like him, tried to throw like him, and chose his number, 7, when I played sports in high school and college. Long after a game was over, I used to wait at the dressing-room door, hoping to see him in person. His autograph would have been my prized possession.

Mantle's image in my mind eroded as I heard of his rather profligate lifestyle and his excessive drinking that led eventually to a liver transplant operation. As it became apparent that the transplant would not save his life after all, the media intensified its coverage of the Hall of Famer's tragic demise.

Soon after Mantle's death, I heard that just days before he passed on, he had told his former teammate Bobby Richardson that he had accepted Christ as his Savior. Bobby's wife questioned Mickey at the hospital, and Mantle replied that his faith had been grounded in John 3:16—which he then quoted by heart. Needless to say, I was ecstatic at the news. If it were true, I would get to Mickey after all—are there autographs in heaven?

I called Bobby Richardson to confirm the story. He related that he had personally received more than three hundred letters from people who said they were praying that Mickey would come to know Christ before it was too late. That means there were more than three hundred followers who, when they saw a fallen hero, saw the harvest—three hundred followers who moved close to their Leader. We can never lose sight of the fact that He loves it when we get close.

Our family used to spend vacations in Florida—not only because it was a great place to escape the raging Midwest winters, but more practically, because both sets of parents lived there. We would drive straight through, which meant that the children slept for half the trip. It seemed sometimes as if Georgia would never end. At last the sign would rise on the horizon: WELCOME TO THE SUNSHINE STATE. Everyone would cheer as we crossed the line. But then a most troubling thought would cross our weary minds: Our folks all lived in South Florida. That meant eight more hours on the road. It felt as if we were there, but we weren't there yet.

It is like that with following Christ. He brings us into the state of redemption by His unusual and marvelous grace. We breathe a sigh of eternal relief, only to realize that we have just begun to get where

He wants us to be. Patiently yet certainly, He works to bring us closer and closer with each passing day and circumstance, closer to becoming fully devoted followers of Him.

When Christ launched His world-changing agenda, He intended that through the generations an ever-expanding band of followers would continue to impact this earth for eternity.

We breathe a sigh of eternal relief, only to realize that we have just begun to get where He wants us to be.

Our oldest son works as a futures trader in the Tokyo office of a large bank. His boss has been eminently successful and has little to worry about financially for the rest of his life. But more importantly, he is also a devoted follower of Christ, passionately committed to the enterprise of the gospel. Christ has burdened his heart for China. He engages in the cause with generous amounts of time and personal resources in that land of 1.2 billion people. For him, following Christ has not meant leaving his career and wealth behind. It has meant changing how he views his position and property. His career has become a platform from which he can strategically advance the cause.

Embracing the cause means something different for each of us. Perhaps a concentrated ministry of prayer. Perhaps a testimony of courage and confidence in the midst of pain and sorrow. Or a widow's mite, an act of forgiveness, a hug, or a word in season. It may involve a mother's behind-the-scenes dedication to the spiritual health of her family, a bold proclamation of Christ, or an unashamed commitment to integrity in an environment more prone to expediency and pragmatism.

For a Sunday school teacher in Boston, embracing the cause meant taking one Saturday to visit each boy in his class. He wanted to be sure they had all come to know Christ. One boy worked as a clerk in his uncle's shoe store. Edward Kimball entered the store, walked back to the stockroom where Dwight Lyman Moody was stocking the shelves, and confronted the youth with the importance of knowing Christ personally. In that stockroom D. L. Moody accepted Christ as his Savior. Kimball had no idea that this act of faithfulness on his part would reap such a rich harvest for heaven. It has been estimated that during his lifetime D. L. Moody traveled more than a million miles and spoke to more than 100 million people!

It was D. L. Moody who led Wilbur Chapman to the Lord. Chapman became a great evangelist in the generation succeeding Moody's. Once when Chapman was preaching in Chicago in 1886, a baseball player with the White Stockings had a day off—Sundays off was a condition of his contract—and was standing in front of a bar on State Street in Chicago. A gospel team from the Pacific Garden Mission came by, playing hymns and inviting people to the afternoon service down the street. This ballplayer, recognizing the hymns from his childhood, attended that service and received Christ as his personal Savior.

That afternoon encounter with Christ dramatically changed the life of Billy Sunday. He played ball for several more years and then left professional sports to minister in the YMCA in Chicago. Wilbur Chapman invited Billy Sunday to join his crusade team as an advance man, to help organize pastors and set up the evangelistic meetings. Sunday enthusiastically agreed. After two and a half years with Sunday, Chapman left the evangelistic ministry to become the pastor of one of the leading churches in America. Sunday felt stranded, but he refocused on national crusade evangelism and began to schedule his own crusades.

An evangelist named Mordecai Ham was invited to Charlotte, North Carolina, in 1934 for a campaign sponsored by a Christian Men's Club founded ten years earlier as a result of a Billy Sunday crusade. In one of those large crowds as Ham was preaching one night, a young man named Billy Graham came forward to accept Christ.

What a phenomenal succession of faithful and stellar harvesters for the cause of eternity. Edward Kimball was simply an unheralded follower who gave up a Saturday for the cause. Heaven is crowded with the results of his routine faithfulness.

CHAPTER NINE

NETLESSNESS

What Is That in Your Hands?

Rachel Saint was fascinated by the stories of missionaries who had given their lives for the cause of Christ. She shared an enthusiasm for missions with her younger brother, Nate. Although she was nine years older and had sparked his interest in missions, it was Nate who first pursued missionary aviation and arrived on the mission field in South America. Rachel had found a comfortable, happy place of Christian service, and she was approaching her mid-thirties when she finally decided to pursue her lifelong interest in overseas missions.

Translation work intrigued Rachel more than any other aspect of missions, so she pursued training under the Wycliffe Bible Translators. Her first assignments took her to the Piro Indians and then to the headhunting Shapras, both in Peru. On a vacation to Ecuador to visit Nate and his wife, she felt a calling to learn the language of the Aucas, the most feared tribe in Ecuador.

One major obstacle stood in Rachel's way. "I hardly knew what to do with this new assurance," she wrote, "for Wycliffe was not working in Ecuador and I had no leading to leave Wycliffe."[1] Rachel knew that if this calling was from the Lord, He would open all the right doors in His time. Her answer to prayer came sooner than she dared to hope when she heard the news that the Ecuadorian ambassador to the United States had invited Wycliffe to work among the Indian tribes in his country.

Rachel's calling to the Aucas posed dangers. In February 1955 she and her partner, Dr. Catherine Peeke, were invited to stay at a ranch near the Auca territory. There they could study the Auca language with an Aucan field hand named Dayuma, who several years earlier had been forced to flee from her people. Although communication with Dayuma was slow and difficult, Rachel began to compile extensive vocabulary lists of Aucan words and phrases.

After only a few short months with Dayuma, Rachel was physically exhausted, and serious illness sidelined her from the work until the next year. During that year—in January 1956—Nate Saint and four fellow missionaries were martyred by the Aucas—slain by the very people God had called Rachel to reach.

For some, the idea of returning to Auca territory after such a tragedy would have been inconceivable. For Rachel, the opportunity of vindicating her brother's unsuccessful efforts only served to intensify her resolve.

But how could she ever break through the obvious barriers that stood between her and the Auca tribe?

Not all fully devoted followers have the privilege of seeing the impact of their labor, as Rachel Saint did.

Desiring to share her burden for Christless tribes with the American public, Rachel agreed to bring Dayuma to the States for a publicity tour. During that time, a breakthrough occurred back in the jungle: Two Auca women had emerged from the forest and were staying with Elisabeth Elliot, wife of Jim Elliot, one of Nate Saint's fellow martyrs. In the summer of 1958, Rachel and Dayuma returned to Ecuador, and Dayuma was able to meet her kinfolk face-to-face. After several weeks of intensive language study with Rachel, Dayuma and the two other Auca women went back into the jungle, promising to return. They kept their promise, and soon afterward Rachel and Elisabeth followed them into the Auca territory, where they lived for nearly two months, experiencing firsthand the Auca lifestyle and perfecting their language skills.

It was an exciting time but only a beginning. Years of language study followed for Rachel and Dr. Peeke. Finally, nine years after the slaying of the five missionaries, the gospel of Mark was published in the Auca language.

Not all fully devoted followers have the privilege of seeing the impact of their labor. But the efforts of Rachel and her colleagues were richly rewarded when at last the Auca tribesmen began turning to Christ. Among them were the six killers at Palm Beach, who told of their anxiety on that awful day in 1956 when they feared the white men had come to kill and eat them. One of the killers, Kimo, became the pastor to the tribe, and he had the privilege of baptizing Rachel's niece and nephew, Nate's children, at Palm Beach in the Curaray River.

In the face of the reality that the Aucas had brutally killed her brother, Rachel Saint refused to shrink from the call of Christ to reach the Aucas. In fulfillment of her dream, the impact of the gospel was felt in the far reaches of the globe.[2]

There are moments that significantly test our resolve to be fully devoted followers of Christ. Following Christ is a cakewalk when He leads us through familiar terrain or comfortable passages. But when followership means that we have to give up something important to us, or it challenges the familiar and comfortable, or it flies in the face of reason or natural instincts, then we find ourselves at a strategic crossroads on our pilgrimage. When responding as a fully devoted follower, we advance to new levels of effectiveness. But when we cling to what is safe, secure, and familiar, we put our followership on hold and face ineffectiveness and disappointment.

NETLESSNESS

When Christ called Peter and Andrew to come after Him, as we read in Matthew 4:20, He interrupted their routines and disrupted their careers. For them, to follow meant leaving everything behind in order to physically accompany Him for three years. As far as they knew, it was a call that would endure the rest of their lives—and that is exactly what happened.

One thing stood between them and following. It symbolized their choice of maintaining the status quo or living a life of unconditional following. It was their nets. If they were to follow Him, they would have to drop their nets. Continuing to cling to the nets and all they represented—security, income, familiar commodities—meant a denial of the call in their lives. But what happened next is dramatic: Scripture relates that "at once they left their nets and followed him" (Matt. 4:20).

> *Followers are netless believers. A net is*
> *anything that inhibits or prohibits our*
> *non-negotiated commitment to follow Christ.*

Followers are netless believers.

What are the nets? *A net is anything that inhibits or prohibits our non-negotiated commitment to follow Christ.*

None of us is exempt from getting ensnared in our nets. It is surprising to note the kinds of nets that entangle our lives and thwart our followership.

He was God's best man. God had groomed and appointed him for spiritual leadership. If you were looking for a follower in that day, you would have known that Jonah qualified for the honor—until God said, "Follow Me . . . to Nineveh." Jonah paused at the crossroads of decision and concluded that he would do just about anything as follower except that. On the rebound he boarded a boat for Tarshish, which lay in exactly the opposite direction from Nineveh. Interestingly, he felt at peace about the whole deal—so much so that he was found down in the hold of the ship fast asleep in the midst of a life-threatening storm. Obviously, feeling at peace about a net in our lives is not a gauge of the correctness of the course of our lives—at least not always. Our capacity to rationalize and excuse ourselves is too powerful to trust anything except our surrender to the call of God to follow Him. Regardless.

As we have learned, followership is not just something we volunteer for. It is what God has built us for and called us to. He has redeemed and designed us to be His followers. Our safety and His work and glory depend on our responsiveness. Therefore He doesn't blink and look the other way when we balk at following; He relentlessly pursues us until we drop the net and get back in the way with Him. As we begin to wander back into the well-worn paths of this world, God brings influences—some subtle, others not so subtle—into our lives to nudge us back into His path. A sermon, a friend, a quiet voice from within, a reproof of life, someone's example—all may be used to tug at the nets.

Such was the experience of Jonah. Like the Hound of Heaven, God tracked Jonah, the wayward follower. He sent a storm to wake Jonah to the reality of His drift. A pagan sea captain was God's next instrument in the chase. Then a random fall of the dice that pointed the finger of guilt at Jonah and forced him to admit that he was from Israel and that he worshiped the God who made the heavens and the sea. This revelation stunned the pagan sailors, who drew the conclusion that the God of the sea was angry with Jonah and thus created the storm—not a bad insight for people without a deep theological background!

At this point Jonah became the center of attention. He was the reason they were all about to get deep-sixed into Davy Jones's locker. In desperation they said to Jonah, "What have you done? [the equivalent of, How could you do this?] . . . What should we do to you to make the sea calm down for us?"

Jonah could have repented, and the storm would have abated. Instead, he told the sailors to throw him overboard. Would he really rather die than be a follower of God at this point in his life?

Exactly!

Of all the things I hate to be called, especially by Martie, "stubborn" stands near the top of the list. I like to think of myself as open, flexible, honest, and willing to change when proven wrong. Maybe it's because stubbornness in others is such an irritation that I find myself abhorring the thought. A follower who stubbornly digs in does not go unnoticed by God. Jonah, no doubt thinking that he had finally gotten out of this tough assignment, was in for a huge surprise. I've often thought that God is a lot like the Royal Canadian Mounted Police: He "always gets his man." When it comes to followers who get off the track, you can run but you can't hide.

You know the rest of the story.

Jonah would become a follower one way or the other.

But he was not a happy follower. When God finally got him to Nineveh and used him in remarkable ways, Jonah camped outside the city in suicidal despair. He had outwardly conformed, but his heart went kicking and screaming all the way.

Jonah tells us the reason for his stubbornness. It wasn't fear or intimidation or distrust or comfort. It was a grudge.

What was Jonah so stubbornly clinging to that caused him to resist God to this degree? When we consider the intensity of feeling that Jonah had about this net—worth fleeing from God over, worth dying for, worth the emotional drain of depressive anger for—we figure that it must have been a really big deal.

Jonah tells us the reason for his stubbornness. "That is why I was so quick to flee to Tarshish. I knew that you are a gracious and compassionate God, slow to anger and abounding in love, a God who relents from sending calamity" (Jonah 4:2). Jonah hated the Ninevites and refused to be a middleman in a compassionate transaction between God and his enemy. When Ninevah repented and God's judgment was forestalled, Jonah was livid with disappointment. Jonah was vehemently resisting a call to forgiveness, compassion, love, grace, and mercy.

Amazing! This wasn't what we might have thought, given Jonah's stubborn resistance. It wasn't fear for his life at the hands of the violent men of Nineveh. It wasn't intimidation at the prospect of preaching God's judgment to the capital of the world power. It wasn't a lack of trust in God to go with him and help him in what was a very challenging assignment. It wasn't comfort, convenience, and all those kinds of things that would have held lesser men back.

It was a grudge.

The Assyrian Empire was a ruthless and violent bully in the ancient world. The Assyrians' violation of human rights makes Tienanmen Square look like a Sunday school picnic. Their total disregard for the dignity of their conquered territories is an egregious blight on the history of mankind. They stood as a threat to the safety and sovereignty of Israel. And they were thoroughly pagan to boot—which alone was enough to make the blood of a godly Jew boil.

Jonah knew of no one less worthy of the grace and compassion of God than an Assyrian. He wanted nothing to do with them. They were his enemies, and he felt they should be God's enemies as well. This was the net that snagged his life, which to this point had been stellar in followership.

HOW FAR DO FOLLOWERS GO?

Christ's specific calls to follow are often dramatic and difficult. They beckon us from the most deeply rooted waywardness. They demand that we literally drop every personal agenda regardless of how unsettling that might be. Jonah was called to relinquish well-deserved hatred and bitterness for a higher, more compelling agenda. His struggle is not uncommon. Fewer things are more demanding than our struggle to love and forgive those who have violated and abused us.

Whether the issue is bitterness or some other tough assignment, how far do we go with Christ?

Followers go wherever Christ leads them—
and it's the "wherever" that is so challenging.

Followers go all the way. They go wherever Christ leads them—and it's the "wherever" that is so challenging. In fact, Christ has a way of walking past all that is secondary and insignificant and asking us to follow Him in the toughest of arenas. We all know the feeling. We hear the call to intentionally commit ourselves to follow Him. Immediately we process thoughts like "Does that mean that I'll have to stop . . ." or "If I really get serious about following I will have to begin . . ." or "What about . . ." or "I could lose my job!" or "What will my friends think?" or "What about my wife?" or "My husband will never understand."

These impulses of resistance are the pull of the nets that snag our good intentions and inhibit our progress.

A friend of mine, pointing to the lines in the palms of his hands, asked me, "Do you know what these are?"

"Things that palm readers study?" I guessed.

"No," he smiled, "they're net burns!"

It was his way of describing the tension of nets that pull hard on our hands.

WHAT ARE THOSE NETS IN YOUR HANDS?

What do you hold in your hand that stands in the way of non-negotiated followership? Let's think in categories . . .

1. People can be nets.

There are several ways that the people in our lives can inhibit our followership. Maybe we are caught in the Jonah syndrome of knowing that followers are forgivers. Acting with compassion toward our enemies is an undisputed expression of the character of Christ that marks us as followers.

Perhaps the net is friends who live, walk, and play in paths contrary to the ways of Christ. While a follower would never desert a friend, what would happen if your followership caused that friend to no longer be comfortable with you? What if he or she was your only true friend? Could you drop that net for Christ?

Or is the net a person with whom you are having an affair? Could it be a person whom you refuse to love? Someone that you just don't want to deal with? A husband? A wife? An in-law?

Prejudice is a people issue. Who isn't "your kind" that you refuse to see as equal in intrinsic worth and value? What kind of people do you tell jokes about? Who do you feel better than? Who wouldn't you want to help? Following Christ will take you to people you've never cared about before. What types of people have you refused to forgive or refused to care for in terms of their soul? We're not just talking about race. Prejudice focuses on just about anyone or any group that threatens our sense of all-rightness and violates our cultural, moral, or religious standards. When was the last time you prayed for the eternity of the doctor who runs the local abortion clinic or the marchers in the annual gay-rights parade?

Our children can be nets. If God calls them to be missionaries, pastors, Christian educators, or the like, could you release your grasp on them? Or, is it too important to you that they enhance the family image and your ego by gaining status and position?

Having served for several years at an institution that trains the next generation for career service in the cause of eternity, I have noticed a strange phenomenon. We have no trouble attracting students. We have a full house every year with waiting lists. Our problem is not getting young people interested in serving Christ; our problem is with parents who say to their children, "That's a noble thought, to be a pastor or whatever, but why don't you get an education and get a real job? You could be a great help to the cause with your money."

Granted, it's tough to stand on the first tee at the country club and have to tell your friends, whose offspring are off to prestigious universities, that your kids are off to a place like Moody Bible Institute. It's not exactly braggin' rights—not in the clubhouse. But it's braggin' rights in heaven, where followers' hearts are focused.

2. Things can be nets.

Nets can be the possessions that have become symbols of our significance: a car, a house, a cottage on the lake, a wardrobe, a body, a club membership. It's not that any of these are wrong if rightly gained and loosely held. But . . .

What if they become more important than financial faithfulness to the kingdom? Or more important than following Christ in service to the body of Christ? What if they are a source of pride? What if they separate us from others in the brotherhood? What if we never want to share them with those in need? What if all these things were obtained through greed and covetousness? What if, in obtaining them, we have sacrificed financial freedom and as a result are unable to use our financial resources to lay up treasures in heaven? What if we have put our sense of sufficiency and trust in them? What if we find our significance in that car, that house, that neighborhood, or that career instead of finding it in Christ and our relationship to Him?

Whatever things inhibit or prohibit our capacity to follow are nets that have entangled and perhaps even enslaved.

When Christ's plans conflict with what we have scheduled
for ourselves, are we willing to drop our plans for His?

3. Plans and dreams can be nets.

Some of us are compulsive planners—or married to them. Perhaps you work for one of them. Planners dream about the future and then plan to guarantee that their dreams will come true. While plans for retirement, family, savings, vacation, or a corporate climb are fine, what happens when Christ interrupts with another plan? What if He permits a health crisis, a financial reversal, a change of career, or a step into ministry? Or what if we are willing to violate basic issues of followership to actualize our plans? Neglect of family, compromise of integrity in the marketplace, consumption with the plan rather than with Christ—all are temptations to a planner. When Christ's plans conflict with what we have scheduled for ourselves, are we willing to drop our plans for His?

Did it ever occur to us that His plans just may be better than ours?

When I was in junior high and high school, I was convinced that I wanted to be a doctor. I caddied for a doctor at the local country club. Our families were friends, and we were often in their home. He would show me through his library and talk to me about going to medical school. Obviously, I never saw my plan actualized. And it's a good thing! I found out somewhat later in life that strange things happen in my stomach at the sight of blood. This malady has caused me all kinds of embarrassment.

Upon returning home from a dinner engagement, Martie and I found out from our baby-sitter that our son Joe had fallen and opened a gash above one eye. We could see that he needed stitches, so we took him to the hospital. They laid Joe on a table in the emergency room and asked me to hold down his shoulders so he wouldn't wiggle during the procedure. Martie was given a chair. I thought, *Of*

course, this is what men are for—to face the gut and gore with courage.
The doctor put two shots of the anesthetic directly into the wound,
just inches away from my face. Something began to happen inside
me. Then he squeezed the wound and began piercing the flesh with
the needle, stitching the gash closed. The nurse looked at me and said,
"Are you okay?" She hardly gave me time to answer and ushered me
into the hall, where she sat me in a wheelchair—in this children's hospital—pushed my head down, and waited for me to recover. At which
point she had the audacity to ask, "Could I get you a popsicle?"

God had a better plan for me than being a doctor. I don't get
sick when I preach. Others do, but I feel fine all the way through.

Much about following Christ starts with attitude.

4. Attitudes can be nets.

So much about following Christ starts with attitude. Attitudes
of serving, caring, humility, understanding, tolerating, and trusting
are all characteristic of the way of Christ that is to be replicated in us.
Yet we have learned to use lesser attitudes to manage our own lives
and manipulate others. Attitudes that consider our own needs above
the needs and concerns of others are nets that entangle us on the pilgrimage. Attitudes that are insensitive, quick to judge, and always cyn-
ical and suspicious contradict the very spirit of Christ. Some of us
have learned that anger is a marvelous way to keep everyone in line.

Pride is devastating as a net. Fewer attitudes are more inhibit-
ing to a follower than a proud spirit that precludes our willingness
to journey with Christ on strategic trails such as surrender, service,
and forgiveness. Proud followers never go with Christ when it means
they may be perceived to be weak or vulnerable.

Changing attitudes often means that we have to reorder the way
we manage all of life. If we have used wayward attitudes to serve our
own purposes and to protect and manage our existence, then dropping these nets may very well leave us vulnerable and our world in
disorder.

But then, can't we trust Christ to help us rebuild a life and create a world that are ordered by attitudes that enhance others and glorify Him?

Are those nets of attitude that you are clinging to?

5. Money can be a net.

Money may be the most troublesome net for many of us. When we consider all that money represents in our lives, it becomes apparent that it is an entangler of great consequence. While some simply like to accumulate money, most people see money as the key to security, success, significance, or the fulfillment of dreams—the house or the car or a Caribbean cruise. The issue is rarely "Do we have enough?" Rather, it is "Do I have enough to do all I wish to do?" This apprehension creates tremendous tension. Money issues are at the heart of wrenching breakups of relationships, whether it is a partnership in the marketplace, a family feud over an inheritance, or a marriage gone sour.

> *Many of us are concerned that if we commit*
> *ourselves as fully devoted followers, Christ will*
> *threaten the treasury. He probably will.*

Many of us are concerned that if we commit ourselves as fully devoted followers, Christ will threaten the treasury. He probably will. That is why money is such a strategic net. When we are able to drop this net, other nets will drop with greater ease. Knowing of the grip money can have, Christ said more about it in His teachings than any other topic. He proposed that trust in great matters is determined by how we handle the lesser things in life—which, in His view, include money. More pointedly, however, was His admonition about the difficulty of serving both money and the Master. We can't have it both ways. We either let Him be the master of our money, or our money will master us.

Bill Hybels tells of a friend's struggle to drop his net of money:

His biggest problem, as I perceive it, is his successful company. Clients whose business he's not even seeking are lining up for his services. Just responding to them is tyrannizing his life. Several months ago I asked him why his heart didn't seem to be as warm toward things of God as it had been.

"Business has been dominating my life," he admitted, but added in defense, "but I'm not seeking it. I'm just trying to handle what's coming in. I mean, what do you expect me to do?"

I suggested he could say, "Enough is enough." He looked at me as if I were insane. What businessman in his right mind would say no to a client whose order would produce a bigger profit? You don't do that in this world. More is always better; it's the American way. The desire for more had a greater pull on this man than his desire to follow Christ, use his spiritual gifts, serve his wife, or be father to his kids.[3]

6. Secret sins can be nets.

The pull of secret sins that satisfy is extremely debilitating. That involvement with pornography, that quiet affair, that other life lived on business trips, that embezzling of funds, that stealing from our employer—whatever it is, it is a major snare. Getting netless may mean confessing to God and to others concerned in the matter. It may mean making the sacrifice of giving up something that greatly satisfies.

> *The nets Christ calls us from are not always*
> *sinful or degrading. He calls us away from*
> everything *that stands between us and Him.*

Mark sat in the pastor's office and brokenly admitted his misery at having stolen cash from his company for the last five years. He wanted to stop and get clean. His pastor explained that to truly repent he would have to make restitution to his employer. But what of his job? He'd surely lose it. His wife and family would have to know. It seemed too much for Mark. He left the office with his nets dragging from clenched hands. It was a mess of potage to be sure, but following just seemed too costly.

THE HEART OF THE MATTER

Two observations are critical here. First, the nets Christ calls us from are not always sinful or degrading. He calls us away from *everything* that stands between us and Him. It is vital that as followers we understand that Christ wishes to introduce His transforming influence into every area of our lives, not just those that need cleansing. Following Christ means that He will transform our view of, and response to, all of life, all its components. It is a call to total surrender. He doesn't ask just for this piece and that piece; there is no guessing and wondering which piece He will require next. He seeks to be the leader, definer, and guide over all of our existence. While we may struggle with a net or two, the essence of our response is deciding to follow no matter where He takes us or what He will require. He is looking for netless hands in a fully devoted follower.

Second, we do not leave our nets for a new career—we leave our nets for a Person. The disciples did not drop their nets in order to take up another job; they were casting their lot in life solely to Christ and His cause. As we have noted, this may be the most strategic issue to understand and embrace as a follower. It is to a Person—to the God of the Universe—that I surrender all that I presently am, all that I will be, and all that I now and ever will possess. The songwriter Judson W. Van de Venter said it best when he penned:

> *All to Jesus I surrender,*
> *All to Him I freely give;*
> *I will ever love and trust Him,*
> *In His presence daily live.*

This is the essence of following. It is not a project. It is a person. It is not a task. It is a tribute to the worthiness and trustworthiness of Christ and His cause. It is that and that alone.

When I choose not to follow in some aspect of my life, it is not the particular task that I am rejecting. It is Christ the leader who is being rejected. If the issue is simply some commodity or comfort that is being threatened by Christ's call, then it will always seem better than the alternative He wants for us. And if all that is involved is my will or His will, we will often choose our want-tos and the comfort of what is predictable and familiar. The issue is a rejection of Christ, and that radically changes the stakes.

> *We do not leave our nets for a new*
> *career—we leave our nets for a Person.*

This is the Judas principle. For him, following came down to choosing between the possibility of suffering and the potential for financial gain. Given those options, Judas chose the money. And it didn't seem to bother him until he realized that what he had really done was to betray Christ. That thought was so revolting that he hated even the money he had gained, gave it back to the priests, and took his own life (Matt. 27:1–5).

VALUES

Netlessness really boils down to a matter of values. Do we value our nets more than the Lord who calls us? Every choice we make in life is a graphic demonstration of the values that drive our lives. This holds particularly for the choices we make when no one is looking, when we are not coerced into doing something a particular way. Many of our decisions involve a choice between what is better and what is best. Compared with everything and anything in life, Christ is best. Always.

Do we like friends? We have to ask, "Compared with what?" Compared with loneliness, we love our friends. Compared with isolation and insignificance, someone may choose to have an affair. But . . .

. . . Compared with Christ, no contest!

And what of our enemies? Can we ever break the binding sense of bitterness and self-protection that comes from an angry, withdrawn spirit? Compared with their getting away with tormenting our life and the vulnerability we'd feel if we forgave them, most of us would choose to withhold the grace of forgiveness.

. . . Compared with Christ, no contest!

Money? Compared with poverty, most of us are delighted to have money.

... Compared with Christ, there is no contest!

Do we enjoy the things that fill and surround our lives? Compared with a life that lacks, we love what we have.

... Compared with Christ, no contest!

Are my plans important? Compared with a purposeless, meaningless life? Yes!

... Compared with Christ, no contest!

Is the satisfaction of secret sin to be enjoyed? Compared with the cost of discarding it, perhaps. But compared with Christ ... ?

What would your answer be?

Every time I refuse to drop a net—every time I refuse to give, love, serve, forgive, go, or change a pattern of living because of something I treasure more—I tell Christ where He stands in my life. I've often thought of how this truth puts temptation into a new and compelling paradigm. When I think of actually choosing to sin instead of being faithful to my leader Lord, the sin becomes far less attractive.

It is a faulty view of our struggle with temptation to think that we shouldn't do something because it is wrong, we may get caught, there are terrible consequences, or we'll feel guilty and ashamed. While all that is true, it is not the reason that we avoid the damages of sin. We avoid them because we love Him more than we love the indulgence.

We don't resist temptation because we think we may get caught, feel guilty, or suffer terrible consequences. We resist it because we love Him more than we love the indulgence.

Would you choose pornography over Christ? Would Christ be more compelling than a business deal that entails an erosion of integrity, even if it meant corporate advancement or financial gain?

Our decisions about nets reveal what we truly value the most in our lives, regardless of what we say to the contrary.

Of course, all of us who are caught up in a systematized, ritualized form of religion are the most vulnerable of all. Rarely will we want to be good for the sake of a system. If we really want something, we will take it and hope we won't get caught. There isn't a husband in the world who will give his life to his wife in loving, sacrificial ways for the sake of the institution of marriage; but he will do it out of love. A good marriage is built by people who value and love each other more that anything else in their lives.

Those who value the worth of Christ our Leader will not take advantage of His saving, forgiving grace. The well-worn routine of relying on 1 John 1:9 won't tempt us: "If we confess our sins. . . ." The issue will not be "I can be forgiven after I do this." The thought that Christ will still love me even if I don't drop the net loses all its appeal in the light of a growing relationship that loves and values Christ for all He is. An authentic follower desires to drop nets because it is a way to say, "This is how much I love You."

Isn't it clear now that a follower is first and foremost a person who is seeking a deepening love with Christ? Hearts that are growing in love with Him produce hands that are empty of nets. Hands that are ensnared with nets are a sign of a heart that is insufficiently focused on the value of the One who is calling us to be His fully devoted followers.

Below the surface, our choosing to hold onto a net rather than our Leader gives Satan cause to defame the name of Christ in the universe before the heavenly host. Let me explain.

Job 1 reveals that one of Satan's ploys is to use the behavior of the children of God to mock Him before His throne. Satan was sure that the only reason that Job worshiped God was because God had been so good to him. According to Satan's theory, if God took everything away and Job suffered, Job would curse God. In other words, God is not worthy of a man's praise and adoration unconditionally; He must buy peoples' favor by blessing them. Job's steadfast refusal to curse God in the depths of his pain proved before a watching heavenly host that God was worthy of a man's allegiance regardless.

When I drop a net, not only do I prove to myself and my world that my Leader Lord is worthy of even my most prized possession; I also prove it before the watching host of heaven. Perhaps more significantly, Satan then has no grounds on which to say, "See, in the real world you are not even more worthy than that thought, that raise, that affair, etc." This, it seems to me, is sufficient motivation in and of itself to drop a net. In fact, we may want to find a few nets to drop just to make the point in heaven and, at least for our sakes, to stop the slanderous talk of the evil one.

OUTCOMES

In addition to being a reflection of what we truly value, netlessness relates to the ultimate outcomes in our lives. Think of what might have been if Peter, Andrew, James, and John had not dropped everything to follow Christ. At the end of their lives they would have had piles—perhaps tons—of smelly, scaly fish to show for their existence. Matthew would have had large stockpiles of cash and no one at his funeral. Perhaps Simon the Zealot would have spilt his blood on the streets of Jerusalem in an aborted attempt to overthrow the Roman government. Thomas would still be a confirmed skeptic.

But because the disciples dropped what they had thought was the best way to spend their lives and took up Christ's way, you and I sit here redeemed. Only heaven will reveal the full results of the lives of these early disciples who became non-negotiated followers of Christ.

We can hardly quantify the difference in the life of a child whose parents are loving and nurturing followers of Christ compared with a child who has been neglected, conditionally loved, and abused because his parents followed their own instinctive drives and desires. Nor can we quantify the differences in offices, churches, neighborhoods, and friends that are uniquely and permanently blessed by the impact of true followers. The impact of a follower's life goes far beyond the moment, all the way to eternity.

> *Becoming a netless believer does not mean dropping one net and being free forever. We will confront additional nets.*

Followers are netless believers who pointedly resist the seductive nets that would inhibit their being in the way with Christ. It's a matter of getting free to follow. Netlessness is the freedom factor for a fully devoted follower.

Becoming a netless believer does not mean dropping one net and being free forever. As we start down the way with path-treader Jesus, the adversary who delights in enslaving us to the nets will offer additional nets. Like a roadside vendor, he will hawk his wares in compelling tones, hoping that though we were netless once, we will be netless no longer. Fully devoted followers leave the path of their followership littered with the nets that they have shed for the supreme worth of the One they follow. With Paul we will gladly affirm, "I consider my life worth nothing to me, if only I may finish the race and complete the task the Lord Jesus has given me—the task of testifying to the gospel of God's grace" (Acts 20:24) and "I have been crucified with Christ and I no longer live, but Christ lives in me. The life I live in the body, I live by faith in the Son of God, who loved me and gave himself for me" (Gal. 2:20).

Look at your hands, the lines in your palms. Are there rope burns from the strain of a net you have struggled to hold on to? Is there a net entangling your progress with Christ?

Drop it. He's worth it. Life is ultimately better without it.

CHAPTER TEN

GETTING OUT OF THE WAY

The Risk of Relapse

Walking into my office, I noticed an article torn from the morning paper and lying on top of the ever-present piles of work. I read with interest and shock of Tom Wilson, who after getting off his motorcycle in front of a Detroit drugstore, was sprayed with bullets from a submachine gun and died in a pool of blood on the sidewalk. The article noted that Wilson was a member of a neo-Nazi gang and that his death was a result of gang warfare. Wondering why this had been put on my desk, particularly since I had never heard of Tom Wilson and had no point of reference for the story, I was soon relieved of my curiosity as the business manager of the church explained to me that Tom had grown up in our church. Tom had been active in the youth group, had professed Christ, and had been baptized. Later, I learned from Tom's fourth-grade Sunday school teacher that he was "a very good student and won many points for faithful memory work, lesson completion, and attendance." Tom's parents had been pillars in the church.

As the business manager left the office, I leaned back in my chair and stared at the ceiling thinking, "I didn't know you could get there from here."

Tom had made a conscious choice to compromise his follower-ship. He chose at some point to determine his own destiny. And I doubt that his first step away from Christ was a big one. I doubt that he got up and stormed out of a youth meeting, shouting, "I'm outta here! I'm going to join a neo-Nazi motorcycle gang!" That first step was, more probably, a choice to not listen to the voice of the Spirit, to love his lusts more than Christ, or to choose a friend who encouraged his stepping off the path. We hardly need to be reminded that had he followed Christ, the outcomes would have been far different.

A spiritual leader, whose moral failure destroyed both his family and the church he had shepherded for years, told a friend that his life began to get off track because of what—innocently he thought—he watched on television and at the movies. Then he took an occasional peek at a magazine. That led to plotting and planning to rent videos. Then he began to go to places where his incited passions could be satisfied. When one of his counselees opened the door to having an affair, he was ready to take that step, too. This sad story of a life inflicting incredible damage on the name of Christ was played out, not by momentary, cataclysmic departure, but by the gradual erosion of a commitment to be a fully devoted follower of Jesus Christ.

These are not isolated cases. None of us is exempt from the potential to fall. The ultimate outcomes of net-bound lives can be told in terms of broken homes, embittered children, unretractable guilt and regret, ruined reputations that can never be fully reclaimed, and an assorted list of additional sorrows.

Any net, no matter how small or seemingly innocent,
threatens to widen the distance between us and Christ.
Sometimes the accumulation of nets can finally break us.

Netlessness is not a one-time achievement. With our hands finally free, we step out to follow Christ only to realize that Satan is slyly offering us another net. Perhaps the net is not a big one, but it is nevertheless a net. It may be the net of a lie to get out of a tough spot, a small indulgence of passion, a breach of integrity, a violation of humility, a manipulative move to position ourselves for safety, gain, or glory. Any net, no matter how small or seemingly innocent, threatens us with relapse and a widening of the distance between us and Christ. Sometimes an accumulation of nets can finally break us.

It is not that fully devoted followers will be perfect. We will find our lives periodically confronted with choices that can put us at a distance from Christ. The focus at that point is what to do with this newly acquired net. When we stop for a new net, Christ notices. Moreover, with penetrating love He puts us in the tension of conviction and reaches back to us with His nail-scarred hands to take the net and free us once again to follow Him. When we hide the net behind our backs and try to follow, we find that the distance grows greater. Tripping over the net, we find that our hypocrisy always slows us down. The farther we are from Christ, the easier it is to get out of His way. When He is not clearly and closely in view, nets seem far more appealing.

The risks are highest when we compromise our commitment in order to satisfy our inner urgings in even the smallest ways. After nearly twenty-five years of ministry, I have yet to hear someone say, "Ever since I became a fully devoted follower of Christ, my life and relationships have disintegrated." Rather, one's struggle, without exception, results from a failure to heed Christ's call in regard to a particular aspect of life. That failure leads to a desire to carve out one's own destiny.

SLIPPAGE IS SERIOUS

Unrestrained instincts are powerful. God allows no room for compromise. Yielding to instincts marred by human fallenness has debilitating results.

In both of his epistles, Peter is unashamedly frank about net-bound lives driven by self-indulged instincts. He warns that God will hold in judgment those who "follow the corrupt desire of the sinful nature and despise authority." They are, according to Peter, "bold and arrogant, . . . like brute beasts, creatures of instinct. . . . With eyes full of adultery, they never stop sinning; . . . experts in greed . . .! they have left the straight way and wandered off" (2 Peter 2:10–15).

No doubt many of us would profess that we have not gone as far as these epithets suggest, yet the basic elements of this description should trouble us. Who of us has not indulged the flesh on occasion or rejected authority when it seemed convenient or taken a detour to follow some driving ambition? Who of us has not dared to risk stepping beyond the parameters of what we know to be right? We are all liable to indictment for being self-willed more often than we would like to admit. Most have flirted with thoughts, if not acts, of adultery. Everyone has felt the encroachment of greed. While most of us have not indulged in unbridled wickedness, we nevertheless entertain the ingredients that make it possible. In doing so, we are all living on the edge of disaster, vulnerable to the risks inherent in our instinctive behavior.

*While most of us have not indulged in
unbridled wickedness, we nevertheless entertain
the ingredients that make it possible.*

He was twenty-five and had already captured the hearts of Russia with his novel *Poor Folk*. Fame quickly went to his head. He drank immoderately and partied wildly. He carelessly criticized the Czarist regime.

You did not do that in Czarist Russia. He was arrested in St. Petersburg and sentenced to death by firing squad along with several other dissidents.

It was a cold December morning. Dressed in a white execution gown, he was led to the wall of the prison courtyard with the others. Blindfolded, he waited for the last sound he would hear, the crack of a pistol echoing off the prison walls. Instead, he heard fast-paced footsteps; then the announcement that the czar had commuted his sentence to ten years of hard labor.

So intense was that moment that he suffered an epileptic seizure—a malady he would suffer the rest of his life.

In that Siberian prison Fyodor Dostoevsky was allowed only a New Testament to read. There he discovered something more wonderful, more credible than his socialistic ideals. He met Christ, and his heart was changed. Upon leaving prison, he wrote to a friend who had helped him grow in Christ,

> To believe that there is nothing more beautiful, more profound, more sympathetic, more reasonable, more manly and more perfect than Christ. And not only is there nothing but I tell myself with jealous love that there can be nothing. Besides, if anyone proved to me that Christ was outside the truth and it really was so that the truth was outside Christ, then I would prefer to remain with Christ, than with the truth.

Dostoevsky returned to civilian life. He wrote feverishly and produced his prison memories, *The House of the Dead,* and then *Crime and Punishment,* followed by many other major works.

Yet his church attendance was sporadic, and he never grew as a Christian. He neglected Bible study and the fellowship of other believers. He began to accumulate impeding nets. He began to drink. He gambled. Excessive drinking and compulsive gambling unraveled his life so that he died penniless and wasted. He left prison with his flame lit for Christ and died with nothing more than smoldering embers.

The tragedy of Fyodor Dostoevsky is not only measured in what he became, but what he could have become for Christ. In the words of the poet John Greenleaf Whittier, "of all sad words of tongue or pen, the saddest are these: 'It might have been!'"[1]

The tragedy of Fyodor Dostoevsky is not so much what he became, but what he could have become for Christ.

Let's face it: It is rarely the large, instinctive moves that put our lives, relationships, and sense of well-being in jeopardy. It is more often the small moments of self-management that slowly but surely detour our lives from what they might have been. Often, by God's restraining grace, we never reap all we deserve but in retrospect realize that we have forfeited the potential of all we could have been if we had indeed surrendered to the call of Christ.

Many parents look in the rearview mirror with regret at the greed-driven choices that took them away from their children in their formative years. The self-centeredness that manages the actions and reactions in our relationships, at best, erodes the trust and intimacy we could have—and should have—enjoyed. Only eternity will reveal the tremendous loss as we realize that instead of accumulating treasures in heaven, we chose to follow the impulses of our flesh and pile up treasures here that are meaningless there. Recalling Paul's words in 1 Corinthians 3:12–13, Francis Schaeffer speaks of many who will be "ash heap Christians," standing knee-deep in ashes before the Lord without any gold, silver, and precious stones that have survived the consuming fire of His glory.

In the same way, James writes that a person is tempted when he is "carried away and enticed by his own lust. Then when lust has conceived, it gives birth to sin; and when sin is accomplished, it brings forth death" (James 1:13–14 NASB).

When Scripture wants to warn us of the downsides of the compromising nets of our unrestrained instincts, it usually uses this word *lust*. H. Schonweiss, in the *Dictionary of New Testament Theology*, explains, "When all is said and done, it expresses the deeply rooted tendency in man to find the focus of his life in himself, to trust himself, and to love himself more than others." He adds, "It promises him complete freedom and liberty but in reality abjectly enslaves him. It is always lying in wait within a man, so that at the right moment he may yield his will to it and become subject to it." Worse yet, "It is clear from [Matthew 5:28 and Mark 4:19] that Jesus considered [lust] as a sin with a highly destructive power."

More importantly, our lust conflicts with supreme devotion to God. Schonweiss concludes, "Only the life that is turned to God's will and regulation and is subject to God and determined by Him, presents the opposite picture."[2]

Living by our lusts not only leads to sin-induced destruction, as James affirms, but also damages the very core of our being, where the defenses are the strongest and where our spirit and relationship to God flourish.

Peter picks up the theme and argues powerfully that we must abstain from managing our lives by "fleshly lusts" because they "wage war against the soul" (1 Peter 2:11 NASB). The soul is the very essence of who we are. It is the eternal part of us where God meets us and speaks to us. It is the residence of our conscience since it was breathed into us at creation by God Himself. As such, it triggers our sense of right and wrong and serves as a protection mechanism against dangerous patterns of behavior. When passion, pride, and self-will are not checked by the control of Christ, our unfettered instincts erode the power of our souls to resist evil and thus leave us defenseless to their whims.

For instance, indulging our unbridled sensual instincts begins to dull the light of morality in our inner selves. Our first experiences may leave us troubled and stung by guilt. This is the war against his soul that David speaks of in Psalm 32. Guilt, fear, and anxiety are the signals that the struggle has begun. Repeated indulgence of our raw sensual instincts begins to defeat the strongholds of the soul, and soon the guilt and sense of struggle diminish. Defenseless, we now find ourselves given over to our whims and addicted to their destructive flow.

> *It is impossible to love God, regardless of*
> *what we may claim, if our life is directed by*
> *unrestrained and unguided urges.*

John demonstrates how a self-managed life mitigates against followership: "Do not love the world or anything in the world. If anyone loves the world, the love of the Father is not in him. For everything in the world—the cravings of sinful man, the lust of his eyes and the boasting of what he has and does—comes not from the Father but from the world" (1 John 2:15–16).

John's point is that it is impossible to love God, regardless of what we may claim, if our life is directed by unrestrained and unguided urges. Lovers of God follow Him. The essence of our relationship to Him is captured in Christ's statement that the first and greatest command is that we are to love the Lord our God with the totality of our being (Matt. 22:34–40).

Further, Peter calls us to be like obedient children in our attitude toward Christ. No one is more dependent, more trusting, more malleable than a child who willingly follows the directives of his parents. Peter then calls us out of bondage to the desires that ruled over us when we were ignorant, and he concludes, "Just as he who called you is holy, so be holy in all you do; for it is written: 'Be holy, because I am holy'" (1 Peter 1:15–16).

David, the great shepherd king of Israel, came to understand the seriousness of slippage. In the midst of a stellar career for God, his instinct for leisure kept him from going to battle with his army as kings were supposed to do. As he walked his rooftop gardens one night, his sensual instincts encouraged his eyes to linger on the sight of the bathing Bathsheba. Driven by the desire for pleasure and power, he summoned her to his palace. Later, when he was informed of her pregnancy, his urge for self-protection led him to craft a plan to call her husband home from the war zone for the weekend. But Uriah refused to sleep with his wife in deference to his fellow soldiers who were dying on the front lines. Foiled, David plotted the death of Uriah by ordering the general into the front lines. This way it would be assumed that Uriah was the father, since no one would know whether or not he had slept with Bathsheba.

To actualize these inner impulses, David had to break through the fences of restraint that had been taught him since he was a boy. God had given Israel the Torah, the law, to prevent inner desires from becoming destructive. The Ten Commandments all speak to the direction and guidance of inner urgings; they set the parameters to our passions. By the time David's self-indulgence was complete, he had broken his way through five of the ten. He had coveted his neighbor's wife, stolen her, lied, committed adultery, and committed murder. He must have forgotten the truth of what he himself had written when he affirmed that the truly blessed refuse to scoff at God's moral authority but rather find their delight in His law (Ps. 1).

David's treachery stayed a secret until he was exposed a year later. At that point he admitted that life by raw instincts had betrayed him. In Psalm 32 he relates the destructive consequences that accrued:

When I kept silent,
  my bones wasted away
  through my groaning all day long.
For day and night
  your hand was heavy upon me;
my strength was sapped
  as in the heat of summer (vv. 3–4).

Although outwardly he still reigned and was hailed as king, internally David was in torment.

> *The best of us can, in moments of careless*
> *disregard, carry nets that over time entangle and*
> *disable us from unhindered, maximum usefulness.*

It should not go unnoticed, however, that in other aspects of David's life there was no doubt unflinching submission to God's directing influence. The best of us who are otherwise fully devoted followers can, in moments of careless disregard, carry nets that over time entangle and disable us from unhindered, maximum usefulness.

FOLLOWERS VALUE INSTINCTS

To maintain a proper perspective, we must keep in mind that our inner instincts in and of themselves are not the nets that entangle us. Our basic instincts were created by God; by His intention they are to be the raw energy force of our lives. But, like raw energy, they were never meant to be expressed randomly and uncontrollably. In the physical world, energy sources such as electricity, nuclear power, and water are governed, regulated, and restricted so as to be productive, safe, and beneficial. Disaster strikes when the controls are loosened or the restraints are broken.

The Mississippi River is one of America's most valuable assets. Its powerful flow transports millions of tons of consumer commodities annually. Its waters irrigate thirsty fields and provide recreation and leisure. The industries along its banks employ thousands of people.

But in the summer of 1993, the Mississippi overflowed its restraining banks and destroyed everything in its path. Fed by prolonged rains and melting snow, the river threatened the lives that it formerly sustained. At the time when farmers would usually expect the sun to help nurture their crops for a plentiful harvest in the fall, they watched helplessly as the powerful floods surged through their fields, leaving an estimated three billion dollars in crop damage. The torrent demolished homes and farms that had stood for decades; it wiped out whole communities; it flooded twelve million acres spanning eight states. Worst of all, the Mississippi took the lives of twenty-six people.[3]

The energy forces that reside under our skin are no different. They were placed there in Creation to help us toward success, beneficial acts, and constructive responses to life and society in general. Where would we be without the instinct to succeed; to procreate; to relate; to love and be loved; to see self as an instrument of worth and dignity that can be given to God and others; to protect; to seek to use our power for the good and gain of others; to take pride in our work and treasures; to desire comfort and leisure; to craft times of pleasure? Life without these drives and energy sources would go nowhere fast; it would be a dull, despondent, and meaningless pursuit. Daniel Goleman affirms, "A life without passion would be a dull wasteland of neutrality, cut off and isolated from the richness of life itself."[4] Fortunately, God planted these urgings deep in our beings so that we could indeed have rich, useful, and meaningful lives.

> *Instincts are intended to be servants*
> *of Christ, not the lords of our lives.*

But instincts are intended to be servants of Christ, not the lords of our lives. They are the inner energies that empower followers to perform to the pleasure of Christ our leader. Our instincts are positive forces when they are managed by Christ's moral authority through the Spirit and the Word.

Effective life management requires that we are willing to yield to a higher moral authority than ourselves. It requires our deliberate choice to make loyal followership the passion and pursuit of our lives. It calls us to have hands that are free of entangling nets so that they can serve Him.

The pilgrimage of fully devoted followers is littered with the nets they have dropped along the way. We should always be able to discern where followers have been by the nets they've left behind.

Our pilgrimage is to be marked by
followers who hand-in-hand, arm-in-arm
form a massive unified movement for Him.

When our hands are free, we follow Christ with hands clasped one with another. Unity is a primary signature of our followership. Christ intended that our pilgrimage be marked by followers who hand-in-hand, arm-in-arm form a massive unified movement for Him. Followers are known by their active commitment to loving, encouraging, supporting, and motivating one another on the journey. Christ said, "A new command I give you: Love one another. As I have loved you, so you must love one another. By this all men will know that you are my disciples, if you love one another" (John 13:34–35). In His prayer in Gethsemane, Christ said, "For them I sanctify myself, that they too may be sanctified. My prayer is not for them alone. I pray also for those who will believe in me through their message, that all of them may be one, Father, just as you are in me and I am in you. May they also be in us so that the world may believe that you have sent me" (John 17:19–21).

Our individualism and self-centered ways often create an ugly scene on the road behind Christ. The nets in our hands—those of pride, arrogance, critical attitudes, and the pursuit of personal agendas at the expense of others—make it impossible to walk as one. Yet mutual love is precisely what marks and empowers us as followers before a watching world.

CHAPTER ELEVEN

FOLLOWING AS ONE

Breaking Up Is Not Hard to Do

For many years our family vacationed in Florida. Both sets of in-laws lived there, which provided an economically feasible stay in paradise. But while paradise was our destination, getting there was often a challenging and frazzling experience.

The screams and tears from the back seat made the journey tense. When our three children were young, the close proximity in the crowded back seat was more than they could bear. The "Dad, she's breathing on me" and "Mom, he crossed the line" kind of stuff exasperated us. We used to drive straight through, all twenty-two hours of it. That way, the kids slept half the trip. Moreover, after everyone was in the car, we would ceremoniously take the "rod" of instruction and slip it under the front seat hoping that a reminder of its presence would create an environment where a cease-fire could prevail.

Division is not just unsettling to family trips. It disrupts every vital arena of life. Marriages, work environments, and our own sense of well-being are all distorted by our inability to get along with one another. If things are not well between Martie and me, it's not a good day, no matter how well things go at the office. If, however, I leave home knowing that all is well at home, even the worst day at the office is really not all that bad. Unified and productive relationships are the key to every endeavor of life.

This is particularly true in our relationships with each other in the body of Christ and His service. While division is unsettling enough in earthly endeavors, division among believers has a disturbing effect that goes far beyond temporal issues. The calling of the church in the world is to advance the cause of Christ and to do it in a way that reflects the power of His character. Feuding Christians do neither. Division turns our attention away from the agenda of reaching our world and ministering to one another. It focuses our energies inward. Tragically, when that happens, a watching world discounts our claims and dismisses the validity of our testimony.

Max Lucado likens our pilgrimage to a large ship on which followers live on their way to glory. He says, "There are many adrift on the sea who would like to get on board except for the fact that they don't want to get caught in the middle of a fistfight between two sailors."[1]

Conversely, unity among believers becomes a mutually energizing force and a winsome statement to a watching world whose alienated and lonely citizens are looking for a place to belong and a place to be loved.

Look at us: Here we are, on our way home to heaven, following our Leader in a pilgrimage that should be marked by a spirit of celebration, praise, joy, and love, and all we can do is bicker. Following Christ is intended to foster a productivity maximized by our togetherness, not minimized by our fractious attitudes.

It is difficult to embrace, support, and love
fellow travelers when we are still tangled up
with nets of jealousy, judgmental attitudes,
gossip, slander, bitterness, and self-promotion.

Paul calls us to a better way: "Do everything without complaining or arguing, so that you may become blameless and pure, children of God without fault in a crooked and depraved generation, in which you shine like stars in the universe as you hold out the word of life—in order that I may boast on the day of Christ that I did not run or labor for nothing" (Phil. 2:14–16). Elsewhere he writes, "You, my brothers, were called to be free. But do not use your freedom to indulge the sinful nature; rather, serve one another in love. The entire law is summed up in a single command: 'Love your neighbor as yourself.' If you keep on biting and devouring each other, watch out or you will be destroyed by each other" (Gal. 5:13–15).

It is difficult to embrace, support, and love fellow travelers when we are still tangled up with nets of jealousy, judgmental attitudes, gossip, slander, bitterness, and self-promotion. Nets always get in the way. And Christ does notice. His Word says that "there are six things the LORD hates, seven that are detestable to him" (Prov. 6:16). A list like this deserves our attention if we are serious about our relationship to Him. The seventh item on the list is one who "stirs up dissension among brothers."

If we do not yield to netless following in our relationships, we are a fight looking for a place to happen. William Bennett tells the story of two Irishmen who came upon two guys slugging it out. One of them said, "Hey, is this a private thing or can anyone get involved?" There's something sinister about a Christian who loves a good fight.

> *The makeup of the disciples shows that they were prime candidates for cruel dissension. We can hardly imagine a more diverse crowd.*

If you, like so many, are tired of distracting divisions, then followership holds the key. One of the most telling signs that we are indeed living as true followers is our oneness. Both the example of earlier followers of Christ and the exhortations of Scripture underscore the fact that *followers of Christ are colleagues in the cause of Christ.* As we shall see, this applies not just to church business meetings, but also to the healing power in the life of a following husband, wife, father, or mother to contribute to the unity of family. It relates to our encouraging unifying dynamics in the office and on the management team. No arena of our existence is left untouched by the blessed and powerful contribution that a true follower makes to oneness. As the psalmist says, "How good and pleasant it is when brothers live together in unity!"

(Ps. 133:1). And in case we're thinking, "Yes, but you don't know the people that I live and work with," we must recognize that the power of followers to unify their environment transcends the most difficult types of people.

NOW THIS IS A DIFFICULT GROUP

Even a casual glance at the makeup of the early followers of Christ shows that they were prime candidates for cruel dissension. We can hardly imagine a more diverse crowd. Differences of temperament, economic standing, politics, background, and culture threatened these first twelve with irreconcilable conflict. Yet they hung wonderfully together. So solid was their commitment that after Christ left the earth, they continued to be galvanized to both their Master and His cause in spite of all that would divide them.

Peter's "Type A" personality would drive wedges into any group. Don't you think that you would want to say, "Peter, for once would you please sit down, stop talking, and let us think!" John, soft and sentimental, would no doubt irritate the daylights out of more focused, analytical types. Andrew seems to be the quiet one; I assume this because we rarely hear him say much, even though he was an active, high-profile member of the group. (If you grow up with a brother as boisterous as Peter, you are, by necessity, likely to be quiet.)

Thomas was the consummate skeptic. If you ever want to have an enjoyable evening, invite every doubter you know to dinner. Skeptics will be obstinate about their negative point of view and pessimistic about the positive points of the conversation and will challenge every proposition that is advanced. And when things don't turn out as planned, they delight in saying, "I told you so."

Think about spending three years, twenty-four hours a day, in this environment and still getting along and working together as one.

There were not only conflicting temperaments, but more seriously, political, professional, and cultural differences that threatened the disciples' capacity for unity. For instance, Matthew was a tax collector. That could pose problems in many settings, but for the first-century Jew it was disaster. These revenue collectors had sold themselves out for their own financial gain in the service of the oppressive Roman Empire, which held the proud nation of Israel in subjection. They collected the exorbitant taxes of Rome and then often tacked on assessments that they kept as their own. No group was more hated and despised in Israel than the tax collectors.

Now add Simon the Zealot to the mix. He was called the Zealot because he was a member of the resistance force plotting against the oppressive regime. Imagine this Michigan militiaman type thrown in with Matthew, a Jew sold out to the very system Simon was willing to die to overthrow.

Throw in Nathaniel, who, as Christ noted, was "squeaky clean," with Matthew, whose very occupation as a government bureaucrat would make him suspect as one who compromised integrity.

Then add fishermen.

Case closed.

Yet the absence of bickering and backbiting is worthy of note. When lives are consumed with the preeminence, presence, and passion of Christ, personal agendas and idiosyncrasies fade into the background. Just think of how His presence with the disciples would eclipse all the factors that tend to create division. I can hardly imagine any of the disciples having the brass to dabble in a little innocent gossip within His earshot. Or think of the nerve it would take to carry out schemes of revenge or to give each other the silent treatment if you were in His presence.

Any divisive impulse would fade with the realization that you and fellow followers were chosen by Christ to be one of His. Christ has a wonderful way of lifting us above and beyond our differences and calling us to an agenda so compelling that followers can't afford not to get along. It is obvious that those early followers ceased to be consumed with their differences when they became consumed with Christ.

Those early followers ceased to be consumed with their differences when they became consumed with Christ.

I find it particularly noteworthy that the disciples, with all their diversity, were intentionally chosen by Christ. This was not a random group of volunteers. The risk in asking for volunteers for a given task is that you just might end up with all the wrong kinds of people. The disciples were not gathered from names on a sign-up sheet. The make-up of this group was intentional. Christ's choice of such a variety of folks obviously suggests that all of us can be followers. It means also that all of us, regardless of our distinctions and differences, can and must be *as one* in following Christ. Since this is the case—since we should expect that Christianity will draw a lot of people who aren't just like us—how, then, can we foster the togetherness that is so critical to our testimony and effectiveness for Christ?

THE GREAT DIVIDE

Every gathering of God's people reflects the same kind of conflicting configuration that threatened the disciples.

The body of Christ includes people who are diverse in temperament, socioeconomic background, gifts, color, and race—just to name a few of the differences. If we could only learn that this diversity enriches Christ's work! It would be a serious problem if every believer were cut from the same mold. In a recent editorial in *Christianity Today* magazine, Philip Yancey wrote,

> Given the choice, I tend to hang out with folks like me: people who have college degrees, drink only Starbucks dark roast coffee, listen to classical music, and buy their cars based on EPA gas mileage ratings. Yet, after a short while I get bored with people like me....
>
> Henri Nouwen defines "community as the place where the person you least want to live with always lives." Often we surround ourselves with the people we most want to live with, thus forming a club or a clique, not a community. Anyone can form a club; it takes grace, shared vision, and hard work to form a community.[2]

Differences in temperament can be exasperating. Some people seem loud and obnoxious; they dominate conversations and laugh loudest at their own jokes. Others come across as rigid and regimented. Still others are so intense and introspective that it drains us just to talk to them. But if we don't like someone's temperament, that's okay. Through God's grace, we can still love and care for that person. I doubt whether Christ was enthralled by Thomas's skepticism or taken with Peter's proneness to impetuosity; nevertheless, He loved them.

Socioeconomic differences can become sources of division. We often think that there is something inherently wrong about wealth and that simplicity and poverty are blessed. While wealth wrongfully gained is evil and poverty may indeed be blessed, neither is inherently wrong or right. As a pastor I was always grateful that God sovereignly placed His people in all the various economic strata of the town. The beauty of the church depends on that kind of diversity. Otherwise, one might conclude that Christianity is only for the rich or for the poor or for those somewhere in the middle. Let's face it, the division of class and wealth is most often ignited by our attitudes: the rich acting arrogant and exclusive, the poor among us covering jealousy and covetousness in veiled references to spiritual discipline and sacrifice.

Differences of color and race are particularly challenging. The pride and prejudice inherent in all of us becomes most graphic and ugly in the face of color issues. I often think that if we are not able to embrace our fellow travelers of color without reservation, then we are going to have a hard time in heaven. Some from every tribe and nation will be there. Yet instead of seeing one another as brothers and sisters of equal worth and value, we see the majority races as oppressive and insensitive and the minorities as whining and complaining about past abuse and present position. And it's not as though we are required to worship and express our Christian faith in the cultural ways of those who are different. We need to come to God in ways that enable us to worship from our hearts and minds. But we must do it without being derogatory or divisive in our attitudes. Repentance and the building of trusting, humble, love-filled relationships are the hard demands of oneness across color and cultural lines.

Denominational divisions, political, philosophical, and methodological tensions all threaten our togetherness.

These are the obvious challenges. Some are more subtle.

Think of the potential for division that is inherent simply in the diversity of gifts. Someone endowed with the gift of mercy finds it hard to deal with the prophetic gift that sees sin clearly and demands that people buck up, repent, or pack up. The mercy person hurts with the fallen; the prophet is repelled by the seeming softness on sin that is reflected in the mercy-giver. Leaders are often irritated with those who have gifts of administration. Administrators are into the process; they ask all the hard questions and can be viewed as obstructionists to the visionary whose primary concern is the outcome. Teachers fault exhorters for lacking depth of content; exhorters fault those with the gift of teaching as being dull, cognitive, and irrelevant. Followers with gifts of giving, serving, and helping see those with more analytical gifts as being far too evaluative in the face of needs.

*In Christ we learn that each gift needs the other to
complement its weakness and magnify its strength.*

Yet in Christ we learn that each gift needs the other to complement its weakness and magnify its strength. Paul taught us that Christ is the head and we are the body, and the head needs each different part of its body to do the work. Can you imagine if the whole body were an eye? (1 Cor. 12:17). Think of envisioning a whole bunch of eyeballs rolling into church and plopping themselves up in the pews.

Mercy people need prophets to strengthen their view of truth and sin. Prophets need mercy people to teach them about compassion. Leaders need process persons—without them nothing would ever get done completely or well. And administrators need leaders to give them a goal to manage. Helpers need the analytical types to teach them about helping where it is important and to save them from the drain of over-commitment. The analytical need aggressive helpers to teach them to get busy in the lives of others.

And Christ needs every one of us to function in our strengths to advance His cause.

Gifts play out like this: If you are in the hospital, the mercy person will pull up a chair and simply emote. The one with the gift of giving will come in with checkbook drawn to see if he or she can cover some expense that you are unable to pay. The guy who walks in and says nothing to you but begins to arrange the cards and flowers has the gift of administration. The teacher wants to tell you everything he knows about what the Bible says about illness. The servant says, "What can I do to help? How about your kids—can I pick them up for school? Or what about food? I'll fix meals for your family." Before the server leaves, he has promised far more than he can ever accomplish. The leader promises to get others to bring the food in and to rally a church-wide prayer effort on your behalf. The prophet reminds you that sickness and sin are sometimes related: How about a moment for repentance? And the exhorter exclaims, "I am so excited for you! Do you know that God often uses difficulty to shape and groom us for a more useful life? Just think of what God is doing in your life. What a privilege!"

We needed all of them to stop by. Christ needs all of us to do His work.

Gifts were not intended to divide us; they were intended to expand our ability to multiply the work of Christ.

Gifts were not intended to divide us; they were intended to expand our ability to multiply the work of Christ.

Consider how prone we are to see our own preferences and perspectives as the right barometer for spiritual maturity. As a consequence, we stand in judgment of others who see the outworking of their faith somewhat differently. For instance, I grew up in an environment where spirituality was measured in part by staying away from harmful, seductive activities and entertainment. One of the taboos was the movies. To avoid the harmful influence, it was important to avoid the theater. This was the case for nearly all the Christians I knew.

As a child, Halloween was one of my favorite holidays—which probably says a lot about the presence of greed in my formative years. So as an adult, long before most of us had recognized the negative aspects of the holiday, I got a vicarious kick out of walking our kids around the neighborhood and then helping them sort and stack the spoil when we got home.

Many years ago, after a particularly successful foray on Halloween, we tucked our kids into bed and called our friends in Memphis to chat and catch up on family news. I asked them how their children had enjoyed Halloween. "How was the take?" I asked, only to hear a veiled gasp on the other end of the line and then a passionate description of the evil associations of the celebration. Surprised, I wondered what they had done for the evening instead. It seemed that denying one's offspring neat little sacks of Butterfingers, Tootsie Rolls, and Good 'n Plentys was a subtle form of child abuse.

You can imagine my surprise when they replied without a blink of spiritual embarrassment, "We took them to the movies."

Too often we are divided by cries of "legalist" or "libertine." Are you strict or loose? Conservative or liberal in terms of your lifestyle? These charges and cross-charges are often fired at each other from the weapons of pride, arrogance, and disdain. In many instances, it's not that some things are right and some things are wrong. Rather, these are not to be barriers that create insurmountable division. We may agree to disagree. We will probably seek an environment of Christians who are compatible with our particular perspectives. We must hold one another lovingly accountable for those things that are clearly out of bounds. But we are not called to be resentful, judgmental, self-righteous, or distant toward those with whom we disagree.

We are His body, called to follow Him undivided.

EXCEPTIONS

This is not to say that unity is the highest priority in our Christian experience. Both truth and righteousness are more important than unity. For instance, core orthodox truth does create boundaries that define and describe what Christianity is in its pure, authentic form. Without that there is in the end no clear understanding of our faith. Many today resist the thought of anything that divides. We live in a world where everything is broken—the future, the environment, sex, family, education, and so on. The resultant alienation and sense of abandonment are immense.

As a consequence, we crave community and resist anything that draws a line and excludes one group or another. But truth by its very nature divides right from wrong. People often say they don't like doctrine because it divides. Core doctrine that reflects the clear teaching of Scripture about the fundamentals of our faith is supposed to divide. It divides truth from error, authentic Christianity from seductive substitutes. And it is not that we arrogantly presume to have the truth. It is that we believe in a God who is true and who has revealed Himself in the truth of His Word. To deny the primacy of truth is to deny God Himself. There is no endeavor more important than truth—not evangelism, not unity. At the end of the day, the only thing we really have is the truth about who God is and how He restores sinners to Himself. That's why Christ's prayer for unity in John 17 was qualified as a unity defined and bounded by truth.

> *Unity is not the highest priority in our*
> *Christian experience. Both truth and righteousness*
> *are more important than unity.*

In a world that says there is no objective, absolute truth, the follower stands in contrast as one who embraces and follows a God who is true and has entrusted His truth to us. Throughout Scripture we are warned to avoid and separate from false teachers who distort and confuse issues of truth. Paul told Timothy that the church is to be "the pillar and foundation of the truth" (1 Tim. 3:15).

Scripture also calls us to separate from those who, after efforts to restore them, persist in their sin (Matt. 18:15–17). Permitting unrepentant sin to exist among followers without censure is to permit an influence that erodes the purity of the pilgrimage. But even biblical discipline is to be characterized by a love marked by true compassion and steadied by the resolve to restore the wayward and to protect the integrity of the faith and the purity of the church.

Apart from truth and righteousness, there is little worth fighting over. Have you noticed that little, if any, of the divisiveness in the body concerns preserving orthodoxy and purity? Our quibbling is more often about personal pride, preference, position, or prejudice. These divisive attitudes must be kept out of a follower's life. A true follower is continually sifting out this kind of chaff so that good fruit can grow unhindered. In this way true followers make a contribution to unity—not because unity is the primary goal, but because their focus on following Christ nurtures the qualities that make followers blenders.

THE MELTING PLACE

America has often been called "the melting pot." The underlying assumption is that all the different kinds of people who have taken up residence and citizenship here have blended into community and live together in harmony. But that is not the case. With all the recent emphasis on multiculturalism, we look more than ever as if we are on the verge of tribal warfare. Politicians have fueled our sensitivity to class divisions for their own gain. Gender tensions abound. Generational differences are more marked than ever. Political polarization over issues of moral and fiscal policy have created great rifts between people.

Amid this kind of cultural alienation, Christ calls followers to show a watching world that He can make us one. The church, by its fractious behavior, belies the spirit of reconciliation and unity that characterizes Christ's program for the world. The Promise Keepers movement has attracted wide interest from the secular media. Journalists and TV crews have probed and searched to understand what has made the movement successful. Finding little to complain about, they are usually impressed by the diversity of class, culture, economic, denominational, and ethnic backgrounds among the men. Yet there is clearly one unifying factor, and that is a mutual commitment to Christ and His Word. There is a powerful sense of brotherhood and love as men worship arm-in-arm, pray with each other, and commit themselves to encourage and hold one another accountable as they go back home.

Followership is the key. The melting place for all of us is the place of submission to His presence, preeminence, and principles. It is only as true followers that we can even begin to hope that all the compulsions to elevate and divide will be melted away. Christ alone gives us reason to surrender our self-interest, our rights, our wants, and our peculiarities to larger, more compelling interests. Christ is the melting place. The power to blend us into one is found only in Him. All other attempts will be short-lived, ill motivated, and disappointing. Christ alone is ultimately worthy of the kind of change required to blend us into one. Growing as a follower is the transforming dynamic that empowers us to do so.

> *Christ is the melting place. The power to*
> *blend us into one is found only in Him.*

In the sixties it was tough to reach across color lines to actualize our commitment to followership, especially if you lived south of the Mason-Dixon line. Clarence Shuler, who now serves as the director of the Black Family Ministries division of Focus on the Family, tells how he struggled with racism in those days. He knew what it meant to be marginalized. As he and his friend Russell walked into the gym at the local Southern Baptist Church in their hometown of Winston-Salem, North Carolina, it was no surprise that they were the only blacks there. Even though Russell said he had some friends in the youth group, Clarence expected that he and Russell would not be welcome. Clarence tried to avoid these kinds of situations, and fortunately, because he attended an all-black school, he didn't usually have to interact with white people. The only draw for him was basketball: *If basketball is going to be played, I don't care who is there, and if fighting is necessary, so be it!*

No matter how much he had tried to prepare himself for the evening, Clarence wasn't ready for what happened that night in 1968. Instead of feeling threatened and unwelcome by these people whom he feared, he was greeted with respect. It wasn't long before he realized that something here was vastly different. In fact, the people in this church were very considerate, quite different from most of the whites that he had encountered in the South until then.

Being with other white kids who accepted him was a new and strange feeling for Clarence, but stranger still was that the youth pastor, Gary Chapman, didn't seem to mind having him around. It was not without personal expense that Gary befriended Clarence and showed as much interest in him as he did in the white kids. After all, Gary knew the risks involved—what would others in the community think of him if he opened his arms without reservation to Clarence?

Clarence regularly attended the youth meetings, where Gary explained how to become a Christian and led interesting discussions about issues that were practical and relevant to teenagers. For two years Clarence listened with interest and admired Gary's Christlike lifestyle. Although things were going well for Clarence in the youth group and at school, still he struggled with the issue of racial tension and prejudice. More and more, he was beginning to realize that the people in the church had something in their lives that he did not have.

One night during a youth retreat, Gary posed a question that Clarence could no longer ignore: "Is your life complete, or is something missing?" Clarence knew that the Christ who was so alive in Gary's life was missing from his own. That night Gary helped Clarence find new life in Christ. "My life really changed," Clarence recalls. "God gave me an inner peace that has stayed with me no matter what the situation. God taught me the freedom of being an individual so that I no longer had to follow the crowd to find acceptance."

Excited as he was to be a new Christian, however, Clarence was bothered deep down by the fact that a white man led him to Christ. "I didn't want to be just another statistic. Later, I realized Gary's race didn't matter."

It was Gary's consistent Christlike character as a fully devoted follower that eroded the racial tension and opened Clarence's heart to growth. Gary's loyalty to Christ over color made an incredible impact on Clarence's life both racially and spiritually. Twenty-seven years after their first meeting, Clarence still believes that "one reason God allowed us to meet was to keep me from becoming a racist. God has used our relationship to break down numerous racial barriers."

Gary discipled Clarence and pointed him in directions that would shape his life forever. Clarence participated in an evangelism training conference and later attended Moody to train for ministry. Now he is involved in a ministry that seeks to reach families in the black community with the gospel and to develop relationships among Christians across racial lines. Clarence affirms, "So many things that Gary does (teaching, marriage seminars, and writing), I find myself doing. I believe I am doing them because of the tremendous impact he has had on my life."[3]

Because of Gary's faithfulness and commitment to being a *fully devoted follower* regardless of race or risk to himself, thousands of lives are now being impacted through Clarence's strategic work with Black Family Ministries.

CHAPTER TWELVE

FOLLOWERS
ARE BLENDERS

Group Dynamics for the Trip

While pastoring the Highland Park Baptist Church in the Detroit area, I was well aware that another Baptist church several miles to the south held our church in less than high regard. To them we were the "liberals" who were not nearly as close to the standards of righteousness and religious propriety as they. Our people by and large viewed them as legalists who were slightly out of date and irrelevant in terms of the real issues facing Christians and the church. A certain veiled sense of mutual arrogance prevailed, with each congregation thinking itself better than the other. We certainly didn't view ourselves as one in the work of Christ. Much to my shame, that never really bothered me. That is just the way it was.

At a conference a friend told me how much he appreciated his pastor's praying in every worship service for other pastors and churches, that God would be honored and His work advanced in their town. Although it was not my friend's intention, his words and the example of his pastor were a reproof to my heart. I had never thought of praying for other churches unlike ours. Had I been too caught up in my own group? Too concerned about the success of our own church? Too consumed with the glory of our own ways? Whatever the problem, it was now clear to me that I had sinned against my brothers and sisters who were advancing the same gospel, serving and following the same Lord.

The next Sunday morning I prayed for that other church and its pastor by name. I suspect that the mention of the church in positive, supportive tones took many in our congregation by surprise. That afternoon at a local restaurant, a member of our church saw the pastor of the prayed-for church sitting at a nearby table. He went over and told him what had happened that morning in our pulpit. The pastor was so touched that in the middle of his evening service he shared the story with his people and stopped the service to have a season of prayer for our ministry. It was the beginning of a special sense of fellowship between our churches and a meaningful friendship between me and that pastor.

> *The fact that we are all followers of Christ*
> *is the beginning point of our unity.*

Why is the oneness of followers often so difficult to initiate and maintain? Why are we so comfortable with our lack of mutual love and concern in the brotherhood of belief? Regardless of the reason, it is a certain sign that we are not living out our commitment to followership. There are four realities that mark a follower. Each one compels us to work toward the unity of the family of God that all may know that we indeed are His disciples.

CHRIST THE CATALYST

The fact that we are all followers of Christ is the beginning point of our unity. If you are a follower and I am a follower, we are one in having Christ as our Leader and Redeemer. There is no distinction important enough to eclipse that overriding reality in our lives. Whether rich or poor, big or little, pretty or not-too-pretty, president or potwasher, the true sense of our identity in Christ as followers of Him makes us inseparably one.

The disciples were wonderfully one, even though they had little in common, because they recognized that Christ was more significant than their differences. As long as they perceived themselves, their direction, and their destiny in terms of following Christ, they perceived themselves on equal footing with each other. It was their mutual admiration for their Leader that enhanced their togetherness. They were struck with a sense of privilege in following Him. In view of His greatness, their advantages or disadvantages in comparison with one another were of little consequence.

When you pull into the church parking lot in your beat-up, hardly-paid-for car, and the posh-pushers pull up next to you in their spotless this-year's-best-of-the-line auto, what crosses your mind as they follow you into church? If it's the contrast in cars, then maybe you're thinking, "If they really loved the Lord, they'd give it to missions!" If you sense that they are followers of Christ as are you, you will have a spirit of rejoicing that what you share in common with Christ is obviously of far greater significance than your differences. What someone else is wearing or possesses doesn't count among followers.

I've been to more than one political rally where people from diverse backgrounds gather to pledge their allegiance to the candidate. It is our commitment to the candidate that unites us regardless.

Think of the ball games where you go to cheer your favorite player on. We talk to, laugh with, and high-five with people who are dramatically different from us and whose names we didn't even know a half-hour earlier. Why? Because we have a mutual interest.

It works this way:

Walking down the street, you meet someone only to find that you are both followers of Christ. There is an immediate bond in your hearts, and as you walk on rejoicing in your newfound friend in Christ, you notice that he has a bookmark in his Bible. You ask, "What have you marked?"

Your friend opens his Bible to read, "Whosoever will to the Lord may come!"

He then says, "And what is that marker in your Bible for?" and you show him, "Predestined before the foundation of the world!"

"Is that a KJV?" you ask. He looks at your Bible and notes that it's an NIV, and there is a little chilling in the relationship.

"I bet you don't believe in the tribulation!" he declares with a note of disdain in his voice. And you find yourself thinking, "You are the tribulation!"

"I bet that you are a Baptist."

"No doubt you are a Presbyterian . . ."

"Could I ask you a question? Why does your choir sway when they sing?"

"Why does yours put me to sleep?"

"You must be a Republican."

"And you, no doubt, are a Democrat."

As you begin to drift away, you hear him say, "How did we ever get together in the first place?" And at that moment you both remember that it is the love of Christ that you hold in common as followers of Him. While differences and preferences remain, it is clear to the two of you that following Christ is the most important thing you have in common, and your hearts and lives embrace again.

You had almost forgotten that you were both followers. With KJV and NIV in hand, you walk on together, discussing your differences as brothers, laughing, weeping together, encouraging each other, and holding one another accountable. All this happens in the context of your common trust in your Leader, Christ.

We tend to think that God values "our kind" more than other kinds, when in fact, He sees all of us as imperfect disciples whom He is urging onward and upward.

Unfortunately, we are prone to think more highly of ourselves than we ought. We tend to think that God probably values "our kind" more than other kinds of followers, when in fact, He sees all of us as imperfect disciples whom He is urging onward and upward. Evangelist Luis Palau tells of two men walking toward the pearly gates discussing whether God is black or white. As they approach, the gates swing open and they hear a deep, thunderous voice greet them, "Buenos días, Señores."

Chemists often use a third chemical to combine two other chemicals that would otherwise be incompatible. They call the mixing agent a catalyst. It is interesting that the two chemicals become one but never lose their own chemical makeup. And the catalyst remains totally unchanged in the process. Our unity in Christ is just like that. We become one, because of Christ, with people we would never have come together with otherwise. Yet we still possess our individual distinctives, traits, and talents. And Christ remains constant and unchanged in the process.

Our oneness is actualized because Christ has a way of taking us beyond our peculiarities, preferences, and personalities—and even our politics. Pastor Tony Evans says it best when he states that "We may all have come over on different boats but we are all in the same boat now."

One of my all-time favorite churches in America is located just south of Cleveland, Ohio. Known as the Gospel House, it was started through a ministry to prisoners. When the reborn inmates left jail, they were encouraged to attend local churches, where they more often than not received a less than enthusiastic welcome. Finally someone suggested that they start their own church—which they did. Today the ministry of that church reaches hundreds of parishioners weekly. The beauty of it is not only that they shelter these redeemed former prisoners, but that other people from all walks of life now worship there. Wealthy executives, former prostitutes, young families, people of different ethnic groups and cultures all gather to worship and serve side by side. This is an example of followers at their best.

I will never forget my first visit to the Gospel House. During the worship, the pastor, Bob Sepkovich, asked any who would like to pray to come and kneel at the front. Many came. As we continued to sing, elders and church leaders knelt next to those who came, in a ministry of comfort and encouragement. They put their arms around these in need, prayed, and listened. It was a liturgy of finding God in the time of need, a ritual of repentance and renewal. It didn't matter who they were, where they were from, or what they were wearing; they were loved and embraced in the body of Christ.

The Gospel House clearly proclaims the truth of God's Word, but there is more, and that is the touch of Christ's love. It is not often that one encounters the unifying impact of a high-truth, high-touch ministry.

When the choir sang, there was a blind woman standing in the front row, next to a woman with a gnarled, misshapen body. They both lifted their faces to Christ and joined the rest of the choir in jubilant praise. There was no sense of shame and no interest in having only the beautiful up front. These women were sisters in Christ, and obviously nothing else mattered. It was a powerful picture of the catalytic work of Christ.

> *We are a diverse group, but we all have one overriding, all-compelling reality in common: We are all followers of Him.*

If we look at all those who are committed as fully devoted followers of Christ, we notice that most of them are not like us at all. We are a diverse group, but we all have one overriding, all-compelling reality in common: We are all followers of Him.

THE COMMON CAUSE

Oneness is also undergirded by the strategic supremacy of the cause. In military operations, wars are won by a unified effort under the singular command of the general. Armies in which soldiers are busy fighting among themselves will soon be routed by the enemy. If the cause is great enough, we will find ourselves involved with, and concerned for, anyone who is enlisted in the fray. Our cause is the glory of Christ, the winning of the world to Him, and the defeat of the adversary of our souls.

As we have noted, Christ's last prayer for the disciples included the plea "that all of them may be one, Father, just as you are in me and I am in you. May they also be in us so that the world may believe that you have sent me" (John 17:21). Because Christ exists in a unified relationship with the Father in carrying out the work of the kingdom, followers who want to replicate Christ the Leader must carry on the work in mutual concern and care for one another regardless of personal profit, position, or preeminence. Our yielding to a clear reflection of His glory demands that we make every effort in our power to get along.

The doctrine of the Trinity gives us the supreme model of oneness amid diversity: three persons of equal worth and divinity, sharing the same essence, working toward a common goal as one. Although they are of equal worth, their roles are distinct and they mutually submit. The Father submits to the eternal decree. The Son submits to the Father and His glory—all the way to the Cross. He sends the Spirit to earth to carry on His work, and the Spirit works to glorify the Son. Where would we be if Christ had refused to embrace the cause by refusing to be one with the Spirit and the Father? What if He had said, "I don't do crosses"? Or what if the Spirit had said, "Go down there and work on planet earth among earthlings? Not a chance!"? The cause would have failed, and individualism would have been to blame.

When the cause is compelling enough, we don't have the luxury not to cooperate. When we are one, we bring a credibility to Christ that convinces others on the outside that Christ really is all that He claims to be. His claims resonate with credibility in the hearts of those who hear His message through our unified voice and example. Nothing erodes the message of Christ more than when followers splinter and divide. The power of the first-century church was grounded in the reputation that, even in the midst of devastating persecution, they "loved one another."

> *When we are one, we bring a credibility*
> *to Christ that convinces others on the outside that*
> *Christ really is all that He claims to be.*

What is more important than the cause of the gospel? Certainly nothing that relates to me or my personal tastes and desires. Needless to say, styles, methods, and personal preferences are not of greater value than the cause of Christ. This is not to say that we are not free to discuss, express our opinions, and even disagree. But at the end of the day, nothing of lesser value should divide us; in the context of truth and righteousness, we prize more than anything else the advancement of the gospel, our love for one another, and the unity of the church.

It was Easter Sunday, and I was well aware that the other church in town had strenuously advertised their services as "Friendship Sunday." That meant that all of its members were to invite their friends to the holiday services. That would have been just fine except that some there began to invite people from my congregation to help them win the "most friends prize." To add insult to injury, they arranged an Easter egg roll on the front lawn of their church to attract as many kids as possible. While both approaches violated my sense of biblical church programming, I tried not to let the matter get to me. Considering the possibility that some people might not return to the fold, it was a struggle to keep my perspective straight.

Before the evening service, I saw a member of my church approaching, and it was clear that she thought she had something important to tell me. She began with a protest: "Pastor, do you know how many were at Temple Baptist this morning"—and not stopping, she continued—"fifteen hundred, and many of them were from our church!" She was obviously upset. In response I said, "Do you mean that in our little town fifteen hundred heard the gospel today? Isn't that just about the best news you've heard in a long while?"

She wasn't quite expecting that. Her jaw dropped. (I wish I were always that good with my *following* game plan.) Actually, I had just been studying Philippians 1, a passage in which Paul emphasizes that in a competitive environment, he would choose to forget the divisive actions and attitudes of others and rejoice in the fact that Christ was being preached (vv. 15–18). It's critical for us to remember that we aren't competitors in the work of Christ. Followers of Christ are colleagues.

The bottom line is that Christ has a way of taking us, as followers, above and beyond ourselves. He lifts us above our preferences and peculiarities and calls us to an agenda so compelling that we can't afford the luxury of not getting along.

IT'S A NATURAL FOR FOLLOWERS

Unity among fellow followers is not a project—and we can all be thankful for that. Projects have a way of becoming burdensome, unfinished tasks. Most of us have basements and garages full of still-to-be-finished projects. Oneness is a natural outgrowth of the process of following. Following and oneness are like arranging dominoes in serpentine configurations. Once you have the design set, all you have to do is hit the first one and the rest fall one after the other. The first domino is our devotion to following. Unity follows in sequence. Let me explain.

> *Unity among fellow followers is not a project—*
> *and we can all be thankful for that. Projects have a*
> *way of becoming burdensome, unfinished tasks.*

By nature we are programmed to divide. With no devotion to the transforming Christ, we are prone to function in intolerant, discompassionate, proud, and demanding ways when it best suits our purposes. These forces are so dominant that trying to rise above them on the basis of our own good intentions seldom works. The only way to consistently counter divisive characteristics is to have a consistent reason that motivates us to transform these inner drives to the dynamics that enhance unity.

For instance, followers transition from self-serving patterns of living to emulate Christ's attitude of *servanthood*. This transition is not done for the sake of unity, but rather because as followers we are devoted to replicating His character. Nevertheless, unity becomes a natural by-product as we seek to serve one another as opposed to using one another for our own benefit. Nothing divides a group more than the entrance of someone who is self-serving. This is particularly true in our homes where division is as devastating as it is in the church. Husbands who see their wives and children as instruments for their pleasure soon breed a measure of conflict into the dynamic of the relationship. Wives rarely thrive when they feel used, to say nothing of the neglect of children that comes from parents who run their lives by their own want-tos.

By contrast, servers in the home say, "What can I do to help?" Their selfless sensitivity to their spouses and children, the sacrifice of their own desires toward the best for their wives and children, the example of Christ incarnate in the home—all make for a coming together that bonds those who abide in a home to one another and to Christ.

Having a balanced tolerance of the imbalances and imperfections in others' lives creates an environment where unity thrives. It's interesting that we always want others to tolerate our weaknesses and to recognize that we are not perfect, yet. . . . All we really want from others is the space to be human and to allow encouragement to grow. Nothing is quite as defeating as living under the smothering oppression of judgmental, intolerant attitudes. But have you noticed that wanting space ourselves, we are prone not to give it to others?

Where do we learn tolerance for the sinner and intolerance for the sin? From watching and listening to our Lord, our Leader. He spent time with the likes of "tax collectors and sinners" and then, when the crowd objected, told the story of a father who, though deeply offended, never lost sight of the value of his son (Luke 15:11–24).

Where do we learn patience with others' weaknesses? From tracking with the Lord as He, with great longsuffering, endured the disciples' shortcomings and tenderly yet clearly nudged them toward His better way.

Whence comes our interest in understanding life from someone else's point of view before rushing to judgment? By noticing Christ's treatment of the woman taken in adultery (John 8:1–11).

These elements of true and balanced tolerance come from following our Lord and His consistent example as He dealt with imperfect people all around Him. If you think that some of the humanity that camps around your life is intolerable, think of how the perfect Christ must have felt about living and ministering among that very diverse group of disciples in their human fallenness.

The compassion Christ felt was always
followed by actions to address the need.

Or what of our tendency to be discompassionate toward others in need—particularly when their needs inconvenience us? Compassion drives us together and leaves residual feelings of love and gratitude. Disinterest distances us from others and leaves them with feelings of isolation and neglect. Again, it is our devotion to the Christ whom we follow that inclines our hearts toward compassionate regard for the needs of others. Christ personified compassion for the lost (Matt. 9:36–38), the wayward (Luke 15:20), and the sick (John 9:1–12), the hungry (Matt. 15:32), and the exploited (Luke 10:30–37). The compassion He felt was always followed by actions to address the need: a word toward salvation, prayer, a healing touch, a restoring embrace, bread, salve, money. Compassion without action is merely sympathy. Christ always went above and beyond how He felt to touch others where they were in need. When we are growing as followers, the compassion that encourages unity increasingly characterizes us as well.

A demanding spirit is highly effective at driving a wedge into relationships. The old "my way or the highway" routine goes a long way toward disrupting an environment. Christ's attitude was consistently one of deferring to the Father's will, the needs of others, and the good of the kingdom.

My father tells the story of his days in the pastorate when the congregation had the opportunity to buy a piece of property adjacent to the church. A wealthy and influential member rose in the business meeting to oppose the purchase. His speech was articulate and passionate. He obviously felt deeply about the issue. Nevertheless, the motion to buy the property passed by a rather large majority. The man asked for the floor. Obviously, everyone was eager to hear what he had to say. He stated that now that the church had decided to buy the property, he gladly accepted that as God's will. In fact, he wanted to be the first to make a contribution to the "property fund."

That was a decisive moment—a moment that could have caused deep fractures in the church or one that reflected a Christlike deference to God's will. Deference smoothed the waters and enhanced the oneness of the body.

Deference decides to yield to what is best for others, for the body, for the Lord. As the country song says, "You gotta know when to hold 'em ... know when to fold 'em." Followers know when to fold their own agendas into bigger better agendas for Christ. That is how we contribute to unity.

> *Followers know when to fold their own*
> *agendas into bigger better agendas for Christ.*
> *That is how we contribute to unity.*

The ways of Christ are unifying ways. The issue, of course, is not unity but rather loyally devoted followership. Harmony is the by-product. We can tell if a group of believers are truly followers by how well they get along.

LOVE—THE GLUE OF RELATIONSHIPS

When Christ was preparing to leave for home, no doubt realizing that the unifying power of His presence would be gone, He gave His followers the formula for sticking together in His absence. He said, "A new command I give you: Love one another. As I have loved you, so you must love one another." Then He made this pivotal statement: "By this all men will know that you are my disciples, if you love one another" (John 13:34–35). Our love for our fellow travelers is a clear signature that we are indeed followers of Christ. In his booklet *The Mark of the Christian,* Francis Schaeffer comments:

> Through the centuries men have displayed many different symbols to show that they are Christians. They have worn marks in the lapels of their coats, hung chains about their necks, even had special haircuts. Of course, there is nothing wrong with any of this, if one feels it is his calling. But there is a much better sign—a mark that has not been thought up just as a matter of expediency for use on some special occasion or in some specific era. It is a universal mark that is to last through all the ages of the church till Jesus comes back. What is that mark? . . . Love—and the unity it attests to—is the mark Christ gave Christians to wear before the world. Only with that mark may the world know that we are indeed Christians.[1]

Loving is caring—caring about the needs of others and responding to those needs with the resources at our disposal. Christ's kind of love doesn't require that we fully like everything about the people we are caring for. It does require that we are fully interested in their needs and that we respond to them, not necessarily because they deserve it, but because we are committed to following Christ and replicating His responses to people.

This is a love that begins at home. It affects neighbors and moves through the streets of our community, into our workplace, and into churches. We know how to love because we follow Christ's example.

Think of the impact that loving as Christ loved would make. He loved His disciples regardless of their weaknesses and failures. He selflessly contributed His time and talents to their needs. He loved them across the barriers of temperament disorders. He loved by teaching, showing, listening, and serving. He loved them with His life . . . at great sacrifice. He loved them with the hope for a better tomorrow, a better home. He loved them by showing them God the Father through His life. He loved them by believing in them. He loved them all the way to the Cross.

Followers replicate His love.

DOING OUR PART

Granted, all that you and I can do is to be the kind of follower that Christ calls us to be. While it is true that it takes two to fight, it is also true that unity is best served when we are all doing our part. Unfortunately, we will often be in situations where it appears that we are the only ones striving for unity. If, however, we focus on following Christ rather than achieving unity, regardless of who is or isn't doing one's part, we will still be motivated to live in a way that enhances oneness. Christ faultlessly and consistently lived out His commitment to His Father by focusing on His relationship to the Father rather than the responses of those around Him.

If faithfulness to our commitment is our focus, then we will never be dissuaded from the kind of life that pleases both God and others. Yet it is important to have realistic expectations as followers committed to unity in a world of imperfect people. Here is a list of expectations to live by:

- Don't expect to like everything about everyone . . . expect to love everyone.
- Don't expect anything in return . . . expect the reward of His pleasure and personal purity.
- Don't expect others to do their part . . . expect to be a follower who does his or her part.
- Don't expect to be tolerated . . . expect to tolerate.
- Don't expect to be recognized and affirmed . . . expect to affirm.

As fellow travelers, we who are so prone to live on a collision course with each other will, by infusing the results of our following into our relationships, bring a presence and an example that will heal and mend our environment.

Expect to make a significant impact!

Followers of Christ are colleagues in the cause of Christ.

CHAPTER THIRTEEN

CROSS-BEARING

The Ultimate Challenge to Following

The other day ... as I sat there savoring hot tubness, crack-
ing small jokes and adjusting to the feel of being bubbled over
from all angles, it struck me that the hot tub is the perfect symbol of the modern route in religion. The hot tub experience is
sensuous, relaxing, floppy, laid-back: not in any way demanding ... but very, very nice, even to the point of being *great fun*.

Many today want Christianity to be like that and labor to
make it so. The ultimate step, of course, would be to clear church
auditoriums of seats and install hot tubs in their place; then
there would never be any attendance problems.... But if there
were no more to our Christianity than hot tub factors—a self-
absorbed hedonism of relaxation and happy feelings, while
dodging tough tasks, unpopular stance, and exhausting relationship—we should fall short of biblical God-centeredness
and the cross-bearing life to which Jesus calls us, and advertise
to the world nothing more than our own decadence.[1]

Bull's-eye! Although it's hard to envision the distinguished British
theologian J. I. Packer submerged in a hot tub, he could not be more
on target. Somehow a system of belief and behavior that culminat-
ed on a Roman instrument of torture has been reconfigured into a
well-marketed program of "let us help you feel better about yourself
and teach you how to enjoy life to the full." This kind of hedonistic

spin on Christianity is a direct contradiction to what it means to be a follower of Christ.

After loving and leading the disciples through the early seasons of their relationship, Christ introduced an element of followership that serves as a fork in the road for most followers. In Mark 8:34, Christ says, "If anyone would come after me, he must deny himself and take up his cross and follow me." He posits a cross as an inevitable companion of the fully devoted follower.

Ivan Minailo, a pastor in the former Soviet Union, tells of being approached by the KGB, back in the Stalin era, to become an informant for the secret service agency. At that time Ivan was shepherding five small, rural churches. The government promised him a life of prosperity and ease and a bright future if he would only report to them every week about what was happening in his churches and what the people were doing. It would be a great deal for Ivan; he could continue to pastor and secure the future of his family, and no one would know.

Much was at stake. Ivan knew that if he said no to the KGB, his reward would be internment in Siberia. If he said yes, he would go against God and betray his dear brothers and sisters in Christ. His ministry would then do nothing but harm the cause of Christ.

Ivan's faith proved to be bigger than the lucrative deal he was offered by the government and stronger than the suffering he could expect if he refused. So it was by faith—not knowing the details but trusting in the God whom he knew would manage the outcome— that Ivan boarded the boat to Siberia with 1,500 other political and religious prisoners.

An explosion in the boiler of that boat took six hundred lives. Once the nine hundred survivors reached Siberia that frigid January, they were force-marched to prison camps scattered through the Siberian wilderness.

Ivan had no idea how long he would endure the hardships of exile. For all he knew, he would never again see the sunrise over his village or hear the sound of his children's laughter or feel the warmth of his family's love. Instead, he felt the harsh realities of his new environment. During the march, his feet became mangled and swollen, and he narrowly escaped the need for amputation. Yet he willingly carried his cross through the snows of Siberia.

COUNTING THE COST

The old adage "There's no such thing as a free lunch" holds true for everything of value and worth. I regularly receive free offers in the mail, some of which are grand and exotic. But when I read what's inside the envelope, it's evident that there is a catch and a cost. The deceit of it all irritates me to the point that I don't even look at the offers anymore.

In the scheme of followership, Christ is up-front about the cost. Following Christ is like going shopping. We embark on the endeavor well aware of the fact that there is a cost involved. Paying a price for something of value is a readily accepted part of the experience.

A friend of ours, an antique buff, recently showed up at a party wearing a wrist brace. On a recent trip to Scotland, she had to walk, laden with packages, several blocks to the place where she was staying. She incurred a stress fracture from carrying all she had bought. (I had to smile—I had finally met a woman who got a stress fracture from shopping.) Surprisingly, she didn't complain about the pain. It was clear that the cost—even the physical distress—had been worth the gain to her.

It has to be like that with following Christ.

If I refuse crosses, then I cannot be a follower;
if I follow, then crosses are inevitable.

Our willingness to pay the price of a cross is the pivotal issue of being a fully devoted follower. If I refuse crosses, then I cannot be a follower; if I follow, then crosses are inevitable. The cost is measured in some of the more prized currency in our lives—comfort, convenience, health, wealth, fulfillment, and self-protection.

The sequence in Christ's call to crosses is important to note. Mark 8:34 calls us first to "deny ourselves." This means dropping every net for His sake. In particular, when it comes to crosses, the net of expected comfort and ease must lay in the path behind us. A desire for personal peace and prosperity must not stand between Christ and our willingness to share in cross-bearing with Him. Dietrich Bonhoeffer observed, "Only when we have become completely oblivious of self are we ready to bear the cross for His sake."[2]

While they were in college, Jan and Denny fell in love and committed themselves to going to Brazil as missionaries. They were engaged early in their senior year. Jan had done all the things that an anxious, excited bride would do. The invitations were purchased, the church was arranged, and she and her mother had bought a beautiful dress. To Jan's surprise, Denny began to waver in his commitment to Brazil. He felt that God may be calling him to be a pastor in the States. Jan, however, was convinced that God's will for her life was to reach the lost in Brazil.

Could Jan pay the price of following Christ to Brazil alone? Could she drop the nets of her dreams and her plans and pick up a cross marked loneliness, insecurity, or uncertainty? Jan's focus on her Savior and Leader was so preeminent that she did just that. Denny stayed in the States to pastor, and he eventually married someone else.

Jan felt the weight of the cross on her shoulder as she followed Christ to Brazil. And the weight remained. There was no one to share in her language study, no one to walk through the cultural transitions with, no one to laugh about the strange and unusual things that happen to new missionaries in the field, and no one to weep with when thoughts of family and friends at home overwhelmed her.

While most of us will not be missionaries, the dynamics are the same. Is Christ worth everything and anything? Or do we value the fulfillment of ourselves with pleasure and ease and live first and foremost to protect our special interests?

In a world that is consumed with peace, prosperity, fulfillment, and comfort, it is a challenging thought to envision yielding our lives to a Leader who may not only require our nets but may also lead us through a measure of suffering. On several occasions Christ spoke of the reality that following and suffering are synonymous. Predictably, after such pronouncements, many who had been intrigued with the idea of being followers left in favor of their own pursuits.

I will never forget the time when, early on in my ministry, a couple in our small, newly planted church brought their neighbors to a service. These neighbors were in their early thirties and had several children—just the kind of family you'd like for building a church on. In those days, a visiting family received a lot of attention. They sat in the second row and liked the message, which on that day was about the creation of Eve for Adam. Needless to say, the text lends itself to some humor, particularly as we think about the dynamics of Adam waking up and seeing this beautiful provision of God standing there in the Garden for him.

After the sermon, the neighbors were enthusiastic about their experience at our church and said that they would be back for sure the next week. And they were. Right in the second row again, with faces full of anticipation for the next sermon. The problem, however, was that the next section of Genesis dealt with the Temptation, the Fall, sin, accountability, and a call to non-negotiated righteousness in our lives. The experience was not nearly as pleasurable. The theme of the proclamation was that God requires us to abandon our instincts and whims about life and liberty and to obey Him at all costs. The lesson was clear. If we do not conform, there will be consequence, shame, and judgment. The family were polite as they left, but I could tell that their attitude had completely changed. We never saw them in church again. For them, if following Christ meant the weight of confrontation with sin and unqualified obedience on their shoulder, then they would seek spiritual pleasures elsewhere.

Like smorgasbord Christians, we pick and choose all that pleases our tastebuds and leave what is less palatable behind.

Most of us do show up at church week after week. But though we come back, we often respond the same way as that family. Like smorgasbord Christians, we pick and choose all that pleases our tastebuds and leave what is less palatable behind.

This is exactly why, in a passage about cross-bearing, Christ compared those who wished to follow without knowing the whole story to those who built a tower without counting the cost. When they could not complete it, the builders were ashamed and mocked. Christ also said that wanting to be a follower and not accepting the reality of a cross was like taking an army to battle without first measuring the potential of victory against great odds (Luke 14:25–32).

The cross-bearing element in following makes even more ludicrous the claims of "health, wealth, and happiness" prophets, who proclaim that just a little more faith will bring you the life of your dreams—or, more insidiously, those who evangelize with glowing promises of a life of great material and physical improvement after redemption.

Life may actually get tougher after a followership commitment than it was before.

CROSSES AND CROSS-BEARING

A cross is the suffering, rejection, opposition, and perhaps even death that inevitably comes from claiming Christ as the Savior. Note that a cross is not a project that the follower assumes as a part of the process of following. It is the *inevitable consequence* of following. Again, the focus is not on suffering, but on Christ. Because we claim Him as our Leader, some of the very same dynamics may come into our lives that were part and parcel of His. If the leader takes unfriendly fire, it stands to reason that those who are following will take some as well.

Some crosses are fleeting things and quickly gone;
some crosses last a lifetime. But no cross lasts forever.

Cross-bearing is *a willing predisposition to the inevitability of suffering with Christ and for Christ as I follow Him.* A cross is any tension or trial that is a direct result of following. If I step out to follow and there is a sense of unsettledness, a disconcerting sense of insecurity or loss, then that is the weight of a cross on my shoulder. Crosses can range from minutiae to martyrdom. Some crosses are fleeting things and quickly gone; some crosses last a lifetime. But no cross lasts forever. Moreover, cross-bearing does not mean that we don't laugh and enjoy, or that we don't have seasons of relative ease when the road smooths out before us. It simply means that no strain or stress as a result of following is worthy of my departure from the way of the One who walks before me.

There are four basic elements of cross-bearing that are important for us to understand:

1. Cross-bearing must be done by *a willing heart.* We are not forced, coerced, or intimidated into the crucible of cross-bearing. We readily volunteer for it as a part of the bigger picture of the privilege of following. In the call to cross-bearing, we obviously have a choice. Masses of people have refused the honor. When Christ said to "pick up [your] cross," He was calling us to a voluntary association with His suffering. Our willingness is driven by the reality that He is worthy of our whole existence. As a follower I come to Him as the all-consuming reality of my life. My one word to Him as I look into His matchless face is "whatever." Because He is worthy, I willingly follow in good times as well as bad.

2. Cross-bearing is also *a predisposition.* A fully devoted follower is well aware that some measure of discomfort will be experienced along the way with Christ. There are no surprises. The follower is ready when trouble comes and not derailed during the experience. David Livingston left Scotland to evangelize Africa for Christ. It meant passing most of his life away from home and friends. His wife would die in Africa. He wrote in his journal, "Lord, lead me anywhere, only go with me; Lord, lay any burdens on me, only sustain me; Lord, sever any tie from my heart or life that keeps me from doing the total will of God."

*My cross will be different from yours
and from every other follower's cross.*

3. Cross-bearing is also *an individual experience.* Luke 14:27 speaks of "his cross," the pronoun suggesting that each of us will have a cross of our own. My cross will be different from yours and from every other follower's cross. Dietrich Bonhoeffer suffered loss of fame and comfort as he stood for Christ against Hitler in Nazi Germany.

His undaunted commitment to followership led him to the gallows just days before the Allies liberated Germany. He wrote:

> ... every Christian has his own cross waiting for him, a cross destined and appointed by God. Each must endure his allotted share of suffering and rejection. But each has a different share: some God deems worthy of the highest form of suffering, and gives them the grace of martyrdom, while others he does not allow to be tempted above that which they are able to bear.[3]

4. Cross-bearing is *inevitable* when we follow Christ. Again, Bonhoeffer writes:

> To endure the cross is not a tragedy; it is the suffering which is the fruit of an exclusive allegiance to Jesus Christ. When it comes, it is not an accident, but a necessity. It is not the sort of suffering which is inseparable from this mortal life, but the suffering which is an essential part of the specifically Christian life.[4]

Initially, we might wonder why Christ wouldn't give us a cakewalk kind of Christian experience if He really loved and cared for us. But we have to realize that the inevitability of crosses in our lives is not the result of a careless Leader who wants to make life tough. Crosses are hewn from the reality that the cause of Christ is being carried out through my life in an imperfect world that is hostile to the One I follow. The rejection, alienation, marginalization, and ultimately the crucifixion were not just invented to be a part of the messianic scenario. They were the direct result of the fact that Christ came to do His work in alien territory that was dead set against His success.

Every aspect of Christ—His character, His teaching, His attitudes and responses to situations—is a threat to the reign and realm of the god of this age. The very essence and expression of authentic Christianity goes against the grain of the world system in which we live. It goes against the grain of the residue of the fallenness that is lodged within all of us.

The inevitability of crosses is grounded in the reality that followers live out the truth and the principles of Christ before a watching world. Our actions and attitudes become a source of conviction to those who do not know Him. If we did not live as counterculture followers, the world would not know that there is an alternative. The alternative expressed in our lives is a reproof to their way of living. Rarely do the people around us respond by falling down in abject repentance; on the contrary, their response is very likely to take the form of intimidation, discomforting and unsettling. It takes courage to be rejected and maligned, manipulated and taunted, yet remain confident, courageous, and compassionate before those who are important to us.

> *If we did not live as counterculture followers, the world would not know that there is an alternative.*

Any thought of a Christianity without a cross is a deeply flawed view of the faith. For a disciple to say "I'll take Christ but not a cross" is to deny the Christ we desire. The very nature of His character and His cause creates an environment in which static and pressure are always possible.

Think of how ludicrous it would be for an army recruiter to enlist troops to carry out a just and compelling mission in hostile territory and then promise that there would be no stress or strain in the operation. More ludicrous still would be for the troops to enlist yet demand that they never be placed in jeopardy.

Christ explained why crosses are inevitable when He warned His early followers of the impending discomforts they would feel:

If the world hates you, keep in mind that it hated me first. If you belonged to the world, it would love you as its own. As it is, you do not belong to the world, but I have chosen you out of the world. That is why the world hates you. Remember the words I spoke to you: "No servant is greater than his master." If they persecuted me, they will persecute you also. If they obeyed my teaching, they will obey yours also. They will treat you this way because of my name, for they do not know the One who sent me. If I had not come and spoken to them, they would not be guilty of sin. Now, however, they have no excuse for their sin. He who hates me hates my Father as well. If I had not done

among them what no one else did, they would not be guilty of
sin. But now they have seen these miracles, and yet they have
hated both me and my Father (John 15:18-24).

Right now, many of our fellow followers are bearing tremendous
crosses for their identity with Christ. In fact, there are more people
dying as martyrs in this season of church history than in all the other
seasons combined.

In Peru, Romulo Saune, a well-known Quechua Indian church
leader, was gunned down by a left-wing rebel group called "Shining
Path." Saune was involved in preaching and translating the Bible
into the Quechua language. He had long suffered threats and attacks
by Shining Path. He told one of his relatives, "My family and I have
talked about the danger from the Shining Path, and we never talk in
terms of 'What if I'm taken?' It's a case of 'When.'"

On September 5, 1992, rebels stopped a vehicle in which Saune
and several friends and relatives were riding. They pulled Saune and
four others out. Saune knelt to pray and then took a bullet through
his heart.[5]

*There are more people dying as martyrs in this season of
church history than in all the other seasons combined.*

In many Islamic countries, heresy laws make conversion to
Christianity a criminal act punishable by flogging, dismemberment,
or death. In some of these countries, the government denies food to
Christians living in famine areas. A delegation from the Puebla Institute visited Khartoum in Sudan in February 1995 and discovered that
thousands of non-Muslim boys had been kidnapped and sent to
detention camps to be "Islamicized and Arabized." In Sudan, Christian men and women are forcibly separated. Children are seized to
be raised as Muslims or sold in slave markets. Many Sudanese Christians have been sold into slave labor for five to nine dollars a head,
then shipped off to countries such as Libya. Tens of thousands of
refugees are dumped in the open desert and systematically denied food,

water, and medicine. There are repeated massacres and reports that Christians have literally been crucified.

In the Quang Ngai Province of Vietnam, the church is undergoing severe repression and ostracism. Christians in the Hre tribe are denied education, food, medical aid, and even burial plots. Church members are warned that their land could be confiscated. In spite of this, the church in that area is growing. One Hre pastor whose life has been threatened says, "If I am afraid of the government, I cannot serve the Lord. They often want to kill me, but I don't care. We pray to the Lord to give us more freedom." Another group of pastors in an impoverished area said, "We don't struggle with materialism because there are not materials for us to struggle with. We are poor and face many difficulties, but God is blessing the church and causing it to grow."

In 1994 in the southern region of Ethiopia, officials raided the area's largest evangelical church and arrested most of its members. It is reported that many members died in jail. They were not allowed to be buried; rather, their bodies were left out to be scavenged by animals. The pastor was tortured, and his eyes plucked out.

In December 1993, Iranian authorities ordered the execution of a prominent Iranian pastor for violating the apostasy law. He had already spent ten years in prison for converting from Islam to Christianity. Observers say that international protests over his conviction prompted his release from prison in January 1994. Six months later, he disappeared and his body was later found in a park in Tehran.

In 1991, following a property dispute, a Pakistani Muslim accused his Presbyterian neighbor, Gul Masih, of blaspheming the prophet Mohammed. On the basis of the Muslim neighbor's testimony, Gul Masih was sentenced to death.

Stories from China are equally distressing. Li Tianen, a sixty-year-old activist in the unregistered house-church movement and well-known itinerant preacher in East China, was reportedly arrested on April 13, 1995, at an ordinary house-church meeting in Shanghai. Earlier, he was in hiding after Public Security Bureau officials ordered him to report on his house-church activities.

Zheng Yunsu, leader of the community of house-churches known as the "Jesus Family," was arrested in June 1992 for holding "illegal religious meetings and disturbing the social order." He is now serving a twelve-year prison sentence. His four sons were sentenced to nine years at hard labor in a coal mine after they made inquiries into his case with authorities in Beijing.

Lai Man Peng, a twenty-two-year-old Chinese evangelist, and four other evangelists were seized by PSB agents and severely beaten in front of a house-church congregation. Then the PSB agents ordered the congregation to join in beating the evangelists, or be beaten themselves. Fearing Lai would die while in their custody, the PSB released him. He crawled several miles in an effort to reach his home, but died on the road.

Majestically, all these fully devoted followers remained faithful to "the fellowship of sharing in his sufferings" (Phil. 3:10).

By contrast, the crosses we bear in
America seem of the balsa wood variety.

By contrast, the crosses we bear in America seem of the balsa wood variety. We struggle with whether or not to write another check for missions, take the consequences of remaining faithful in the marketplace, or bear the intimidation of being known as a Christian among our associates—while our fellow travelers shed their blood. Their crosses are obvious. What kinds of crosses are we called to bear?

KNOWING A CROSS WHEN WE SEE ONE

The first cross we bear may consist of the struggle to extract ourselves from the habits and involvements of a lifestyle developed before we became followers. Addictions of all kinds—from drugs to food to other kinds of self-indulgence—create a hunger that can last a lifetime. The temptation to reclaim these nets that once soothed and satisfied will often cause great agony of heart, mind, body, and soul.

Another cross may be the turbulence that is caused in relationships as our lives begin to change under the transforming work of the

Spirit. People close to us are used to living with us the way we were. I am surprised how often, for example, a person who begins to change for the better at home meets more resistance than encouragement from spouse and family. The reason is simply that those who live around us develop their own systems of responding to our weaknesses and imperfections. If a cross-bearer starts to shape up, those around him or her feel as if they have to shape up too. Guilt surfaces along with the unspoken pressure to change. Instead of adjusting, those around us will often give us grief, hoping to intimidate us back into the old system.

There are the crosses of loneliness and alienation arising from the potential loss of friends who have been important to us in the past. While we would never reject them, they may very well reject us when they realize that our values and life perspectives not only contradict theirs but implicitly condemn their lifestyle.

Sometimes the cross is the pressure we feel in trying to extract ourselves from patterns in the marketplace that have served us and our colleagues well. It's tough to tell the guy you work with, "I don't do it that way any more."

It is a cross experience to go back to those we have cheated and offended, to make restitution for our actions before we became followers.

There is no place in followership for self-inflicted crosses. Looking for crosses so that we can appear to be more committed is not a virtue.

But there is no place in followership for self-inflicted crosses. Looking for crosses so that we can appear to be more committed is not a virtue. There is no merit in bearing a cross that we have constructed through our own waywardness. If people reject me because I am a social bulldozer, it's not a cross; it's a consequence of carelessness and sin, and I need to change my ways and find patterns of relating that are productive and satisfying. As Peter says, "But how is it to your credit if you receive a beating for doing wrong and endure it?" (1 Peter 2:20).

Crosses are not just any kind of suffering. They are what comes as direct result of a choice to follow Christ. The next time we get a cold or suffer a financial setback in the normal course of business, we are not picking up a cross.

Crosses come as a direct result of our commitment to follow.

Bob knew that he could no longer be a fully devoted follower and stay in his present career. His cross involved the decision to leave his rapid ascent in the company for the insecure vistas of another job in another place.

When their only daughter was called as a single to go to the Ukraine as a missionary, the Harshaws took it as a natural consequence of following to release her with their enthusiastic support even though their hearts would bear the painful cross of separation.

Sheri and a friend were the only followers of Christ in their school. The taunts of "they're virgins" and "you've got to be kidding" that often came when their lifestyle was out of sync with other teenagers comprised their cross. Theirs was the cross of identity with a Christ who Himself was marginalized and misunderstood.

LAYING OUR BURDENS DOWN

Unfortunately, when the pressure increases, we are tempted to lay our cross down and deny Him for our own comfort and sense of well-being. Peter's encounter with the enemies of Christ around the fire the night before the crucifixion is a classic case. Accused of being one of Christ's followers, Peter denied that he even knew Him. It's as if he said, "What was that you asked? Excuse me while I set this cross down.... A follower of Christ, you ask? Not me. You must be confusing me with someone else." And then the cock crowed, and Peter's heart sickened that he had been intimidated into laying down his cross.

In Oxford, England, there is a grand statue commemorating three reformers who gave their lives to the fire for Christ: Hugh Latimer, Nicholas Ridley, and Thomas Cranmer. Cranmer, who at that time was the archbishop of Canterbury, was forced to watch Latimer and Ridley be burned at the stake in October 1555. As the fires were lit, Latimer cried out his now-famous words, "Be of good comfort, Master Ridley, and play the man. We shall this day light such a candle by God's grace in England as I trust shall never be put out!"

Although Cranmer was impressed with his friends' courage, his fear of being burned at the stake caused him to sign a bill of recantment, saving his own life while denying His Christ. It's as though he said, "Enough is enough," and set his cross down. Distraught at reneging on his call to cross-bearing, he later returned to the authorities and publicly recanted his recantation. As he was led to the stake, he held out his hand and asked that it be burned first, since it was the hand that had betrayed His Lord in the signing of the document. He suffered martyrdom on March 21, 1556.

Whether light or heavy, the crosses of loyally devoted followers are never set down. As we walk in the way with Him, we note the deep rut that gouges the path before us and we are reminded that Christ carved that rut with the cross He bore. When we see Him crucified for us, we gladly say, "I have been crucified with Christ and I no longer live, but Christ lives in me. The life I live in the body, I live by faith in the Son of God, who loved me and gave himself for me" (Gal. 2:20).

ISN'T THERE SOMETHING BETTER?

Crosses must always be seen in the balance of a life with Jesus Christ that has its seasons of joy, satisfaction, and relatively painless experiences. That reality helps to cushion the weight of a cross, but it is also the case that as we lift our eyes, down the road there will be realities beyond the moment of the cross that will encourage us.

Cross-bearing must always be seen in the perspective of the long view. There is something better for us than just a cross—something eternally better.

Cross-bearing must always be seen in the perspective of the long view. There is something better for us than just a cross—something eternally better. God never intended that this present world would be all we have. Indeed, given the Fall and the curse that followed it, we should not expect much here. We have somehow come to believe that this world is where maximum peace and happiness should be enjoyed. We have either not known or have forgotten that this nasty, brutish world is of short duration, and fullness and happiness will be our guaranteed experience in the world to come. One scholar has suggested that if we knew the extent of the Fall, we'd be surprised that anything good happens at all in this life.

Fortunately, the cross-bearing follower knows that God has planned a far better place where there is no suffering, sorrow, or pain. At the border there is a sign that says, "Check your crosses here. Unnecessary for the future. Forever."

Both James and John wrote that there is a crown of life awaiting those who have suffered on Christ's behalf (James 1:12; Rev. 2:10).

Christ has this long view in mind when He issues the call to cross-bearing. He taught, "For whoever wants to save his life will lose it, but whoever loses his life for me and for the gospel will save it" (Mark 8:35). As Scripture demonstrates, on the other side of suffering and loss is the certainty of glory and gain.

Cross-bearing is like surgery. No one would ever volunteer for surgery just to have the experience. Surgery becomes necessary to the bigger picture of good health and longevity. As painful as it is, we willingly accept it and endure it with a good spirit because we are convinced of the cause and the bright prospects on the other side of the pain.

BUT UNTIL THEN ...

There are five realities that provide the strength for us to carry our crosses well.

1. There is the more-than-sufficient grace of God to enable us to carry what He has required. He never requires more than we can bear. He provides His supernatural resources when He asks us to bear a cross (1 Cor. 10:13; 2 Cor. 12:9).

2. Christ will be present in the crisis of our cross. He promises, "Never will I leave you; never will I forsake you" (Heb. 13:5). You may have heard the story of the person who went to heaven after a life filled with heavy crosses. Christ showed him a beach with two sets of footprints that tracked along the water's edge. Christ said, "This is your life and, as you can see, I walked all the way with you." Seeing a stretch where there was only one set of footprints, the suf-

fering saint replied, "But look, that was the toughest time of my life and you were gone."

"No," Christ replied, "that's where I picked you up and carried you."

The reality that Christ suffered in every way that we might have to suffer guarantees His sensitive, caring response to us.

3. Knowing that our Lord carried every kind of cross that we will ever be asked to carry assures us that we are not alone and that He is fully aware of the weight and trauma of the cross. He was displaced and suffered loss of fame, fortune, and acclaim. He was rejected, lonely, misunderstood, afflicted physically, mentally, emotionally, and spiritually as a consequence of following His Father. This reality compelled Paul to say that he longed to know Christ as completely as possible, including an acquaintance with the fellowship of his sufferings (Phil. 3:10). The reality that Christ suffered in every way that we might have to suffer guarantees His sensitive, caring response to us.

> For we do not have a high priest who is unable to sympathize with our weaknesses, but we have one who has been tempted in every way, just as we are—yet was without sin. Let us then approach the throne of grace with confidence, so that we may receive mercy and find grace to help us in our time of need (Heb. 4:15-16).

4. There is a special and certain reward for those who are willing to suffer for and with Christ. To the believers at Smyrna, Christ said, "Do not be afraid of what you are about to suffer. I tell you, the devil will put some of you in prison to test you, and you will suffer persecution for ten days. Be faithful, even to the point of death, and I will give you the crown of life" (Rev. 2:10). Throughout the book of Revelation, martyrs and those who have suffered greatly are given special notice and stature. John writes,

> Then one of the elders asked me, "These in white robes— who are they, and where did they come from?"

I answered, "Sir, you know."

And he said, "These are they who have come out of the great tribulation; they have washed their robes and made them white in the blood of the Lamb. Therefore,

> "they are before the throne of God
>> and serve him day and night in his temple;
> and he who sits on the throne will spread his tent over
>> them.
> Never again will they hunger;
>> never again will they thirst.
> The sun will not beat upon them,
>> nor any scorching heat.
> For the Lamb at the center of the throne will be their
>> shepherd;
>> he will lead them to springs of living water.
> And God will wipe away every tear from their eyes."

(Rev. 7:13-17)

As a boy I often sang these words from a well-known hymn:

> *It will be worth it all*
> *When we see Jesus,*
> *Life's trials will seem so small*
> *When we see Christ;*
> *One glimpse of His dear face*
> *All sorrows will erase,*
> *So bravely run the race*
> *Till we see Christ.*

5. There is the companionship of fellow cross-bearers who provide encouragement and mutual support. Just as Simon the Cyrene came alongside Christ when His cross became unbearably heavy, so it is often our privilege to become fellow cross-bearers with brothers or sisters who are enduring suffering for Christ's sake.

THE GLORY AND THE GAIN

A friend of mine is fond of saying, "God never wastes our sorrows." His statement is supported both by the love of God and by a myriad of scriptural attestations and historical events. It is the truth that God works all things together for good (Rom. 8:28). It is the reality that after the cross there was an empty tomb. God is not a God of half-finished projects. He completes our sorrows with the intended outcomes of His glory, the gain of His kingdom, and our ultimate good. When He knows that the only way to accomplish strategic eternal purposes is through the suffering of His church and His followers, He empowers them through the pain and then rewards and refreshes them afterward in His own way and time.

> *"God never wastes our sorrows."*
> *He works all things together for good.*

Jan left the side of her fiance to follow Christ to Brazil—alone. For years she gladly served the Lord, her Leader—alone. Then one day her eyes caught the eyes of a widower missionary who had several children. They fell wonderfully in love. The rest is history—instant family! In His time, God lifted the cross and rewarded His follower.

Amid the arduous circumstances in Siberia, Ivan and the many fully devoted followers of Christ sentenced with him gathered on a regular basis for prayer and worship. Their joy could not be squelched. Their zeal for Christ reached beyond their persecution. The government's efforts to marginalize their impact for Christ did not curtail their commitment to the call. In fact, the government actually afforded them a unique opportunity to advance the cause of Christ. Groups of prisoners were sent out all over Siberia to help build the towns for Stalin's regime. A carpenter by trade, Ivan was a useful craftsman in this endeavor. But in this, he also helped to establish cell groups of believers in those remote villages. He reports that "today there are many, many churches all over Siberia that proclaim the gospel of Jesus Christ—a direct result of those prisoner groups that met in those towns throughout Siberia."

After ten years of labor, Ivan was released. He knew that it had been worth it all—worth the risk to follow the call of Christ, to remain committed to that call, and to spread the impact of Christ's life and love throughout that desolate land.

Now Ivan continues to pastor five small rural churches in the countryside of the former Soviet Union, and the impact of his life as a fully devoted follower is still being realized.

Christ concluded His ministry to the disciples with these strengthening words: "I have told you these things, so that in me you may have peace. In this world you will have trouble. But take heart! I have overcome the world" (John 16:33).

But ...

Cross-bearing doesn't always end "happily ever after" in this life. Yet Christ, who is the author and finisher of our faith, writes a glorious last chapter for our lives. For some of us, that ending may be when we get to heaven and hear Him say, "Well done, good and faithful servant." For others, in the same way that Paul bore his health problems, it may be the reward of seeing God's handiwork more powerfully through our cross than we would have seen without the cross. Whether Christ culminates our crosses in release, refreshment, or reward, one thing remains sure, and that is that He schedules crosses for glory, gain, and good.

The light at the end of our cross-bearing tunnel is the assured reality of His character, resolve, and power to bring it all to His good and glorious intended purpose. We don't need to know the outcome; we only need to know the reliability of the One we are following into the storm.

John and Betty Stam were both fully devoted followers in their own right. Long before they literally surrendered their lives to the hands of Communist guerrilla leaders in China in the mid-1930s, they had surrendered their lives to the cause of Christ—regardless, wherever He would lead them, whatever would befall them. They were committed to following Christ, and they knew that there could be risks involved and some loss of personal pleasure and gain.

The pattern of followership in their lives was already evident in their college days at Moody Bible Institute, where they met and fell in love. Betty and John's future ambitions were pointing in the same direction, but the desire for marriage was seen as secondary.

To his father, John wrote, "Betty knows that, in all fairness and love to her, I cannot ask her to enter into an engagement with years to wait.... The China Inland Mission has appealed for men, single men, to itinerate in sections where it would be almost impossible to take a woman.... Some time ago I promised the Lord that, if fitted for this forward movement, I would gladly go into it, so now I cannot back down without sufficient reason, merely upon personal considerations."

The daughter of Presbyterian missionaries to China, Betty sailed back to China in the fall of 1931, on completion of her studies, while John remained at Moody to finish his senior year. As the class speaker for his graduation ceremony, John challenged his fellow students to go forward with the task of world evangelism: "Let us remind ourselves that the Great Commission was never qualified by clauses calling for advance only if funds were plentiful and no hardship or self-denial involved [*sic*]. On the contrary, we are told to expect tribulation and even persecution, but with it victory in Christ."

There was reason to expect persecution. The situation in China was very grim, with frequent acts of violence against missions being reported.

> *"Let us remind ourselves that the Great Commission was never qualified by clauses calling for advance only if funds were plentiful and no hardship or self-denial involved."*

After his graduation, John sailed for China, excited about his future ministry but not expecting to see Betty. Just before he arrived in China, she was forced to return to Shanghai for medical reasons, and there she and John had an unexpected but joyful reunion that resulted in their engagement.

In September 1934, after they had been married nearly a year and had just given birth to a baby girl, John and Betty were assigned to a station in the province of Anhwei, where missionaries had been evacuated two years earlier. Communist activity, they were told, had diminished, and both CIM and the local magistrate guaranteed their safety.

Unfortunately, they had seriously misjudged the situation. The Stams arrived at the end of November, and before the first week of December had passed, they had been attacked in their home by Communist soldiers. Though placed under heavy guard, John was permitted to send a letter to his superiors:

Tsingteh, An.

Dec. 6, 1934

China Inland Mission,
Shanghai.

Dear Brethren,

My wife, baby and myself are today in the hands of the Communists, in the city of Tsingteh. Their demand is twenty thousand dollars for our release.

All our possessions and stores are in their hands, but we praise God for peace in our hearts and a meal tonight. God grant you wisdom in what you do, and us fortitude, courage and peace of heart. He is able—and a wonderful Friend in such a time.

Things happened so quickly this a.m. They were in the city just a few hours after the ever-persistent rumors really became alarming, so that we could not prepare to leave in time. We were just too late.

The Lord bless and guide you, and as for us, may God be glorified whether by life or by death.

In Him,
John C. Stam[6]

The day after the letter was written, the Stams were forced to make a grueling march to another town. After they arrived at their destination, they were stripped of their outer clothes and paraded through the streets and publicly ridiculed, while the Communist guerrilla leaders urged the townspeople to come out in full force to view the execution.

Although their baby girl was spared and secretly delivered into the hands of another missionary family, it seemed that for John and Betty, all was lost. The Stams had only spent a short time in China, and their efforts to advance the cause of Christ had barely gotten off the ground. But they followed Christ regardless, knowing that as long as they were faithful, He would be glorified whether it be through their life or their death.

Found among their things was this poem, one of Betty's favorites and written by E. H. Hamilton:

> *Afraid? Of What?*
> *To feel the spirit's glad release?*
> *To pass from pain to perfect peace,*
> *The strife and strain of life to cease?*
> *Afraid—of that?*
>
> *Afraid? Of What?*
> *Afraid to see the Savior's face?*
> *To hear His welcome, and to trace*
> *The glory gleam from wounds of grace?*
> *Afraid—of that?*
>
> *Afraid? Of What?*
> *A flash—a crash—a pierced heart!*
> *Darkness—light—O heaven's art!*
> *Each wound of His a counterpart!*
> *Afraid—of that?*
>
> *Afraid? Of What?*
> *To do by death what life could not?*
> *Baptize with blood a stony plot*
> *Till souls shall blossom from the spot?*
> *Afraid—of that?*[7]

These lines express perfectly the mindset (or the heartset) of a fully devoted follower who is willing to go anywhere—whatever. And while it is easy to speculate what could have been accomplished through the lives of John and Betty Stam, their martyrdom had far-reaching effects for the cause of Christ. Many young people, inspired by the Stams' sacrifice, dedicated their lives to missions, and the year 1935 saw the greatest amount of money come into China Inland Mission since the stock market crash in 1929.[8]

The story of the Stams' willingness to bear the cross of death for the cause of Christ became legendary among the remnant of Chinese Christians. Their testimony became a model for the severe suffering and oppression that believers faced through the subsequent decades in China. As they bore their crosses, God was miraculously expanding their capacity to reach their land for Christ. By the time all foreign missionaries were expelled by the Communists in 1949-50, there were an estimated one million believers in that country. Today, as the door begins to crack open again, the estimates are that there are more than seventy million believers in China who are faithful to His cause. There is no doubt that the cross of the Stams and others like them released the resurrection power of the gospel to be spread in unprecedented ways without outside help.

Indeed, their death did what life could not as they baptized with blood a stony plot and millions of souls blossomed from that spot.

If following doesn't embrace the long view and keep the God of ultimate conclusions in clear view, then crosses will indeed become unbearable and irrelevant.

Those who follow Christ never pay a price—
not really. They invest the weight of their cross in the glory
of the King and the gain of His everlasting kingdom.

Isaac Watts posed the call of a follower well when he wrote:

Am I a soldier of the cross,
A follower of the Lamb?
And shall I fear to own His cause
Or blush to speak His name?

Must I be carried to the skies
On flowery beds of ease,
While others fought to win the prize
And sailed through bloody seas?

Are there no foes for me to face?
Must I not stem the flood?

Is this vile world a friend to grace,
To help me on to God?

Sure I must fight if I would reign—
Increase my courage, Lord!
I'll bear the toil, endure the pain,
Supported by Thy Word.

Those who follow Christ never pay a price—not really. They invest the weight of their cross in the glory of the King and the gain of His everlasting kingdom.

NOTES

Chapter One: Follow the Leader

[1]F. B. Meyer, *The Shepherd Psalm* (London: Morgan & Scott, n.d.), 120–21.
[2]Robert Kelley, *The Power of Followership* (New York: Doubleday, 1992), 12.
[3]Dietrich Bonhoeffer, *The Cost of Discipleship* (New York: Touchstone, 1995), 59.
[4]William Barclay, ed., *The Daily Study Bible*, "The Revelation of John," vol. 1 (Philadelphia: Westminster Press), 94.

Chapter Two: Life the Way It Was Meant to Be

[1]Garry Wills, *Certain Trumpets: The Call of Leaders* (New York: Simon & Schuster, 1994), 13.
[2]Douglas Coupland, *Life After God* (New York: Simon & Schuster/Pocket Books, 1995), 359.
[3]Julius Lester, *The Chronicle of Higher Education*, 16 February 1996, B5.
[4]"Generation X Spells Out What's Important to It," *USA Today*, 30 October 1995, 6D.

Chapter Three: The Follower in All of Us

[1]Francis Thompson, *The Hound of Heaven* (New York: McCracken Press, 1993).
[2]*Time*, 29 August 1994, 39.
[3]E. Stanley Jones, "In Christ" (Source unknown).
[4]Lewis Carroll, *Alice's Adventures in Wonderland and Through the Looking Glass* (New York: New American Library, 1960), 62.

Chapter Four: The Tyranny of Self-Directed Living

[1]William J. Bennett, *The Book of Virtues: A Treasury of Great Moral Stories* (New York: Simon & Schuster, 1993), 48.
[2]David Wells, "Our Dying Culture," chap. 1 in *The Formal Papers of the Alliance of Confessing Evangelicals' Summit*, 17–20 April 1996, 3–4.
[3]Robert Bork, "Hard Truths About the Culture War," *First Things* (June/July 1995), 18–19.
[4]Quoted in Wells, "Our Dying Culture," 9.

Chapter Five: The Compelling Christ

[1]Charles W. Colson, *Kingdoms in Conflict* (Grand Rapids: Zondervan, 1987), 85.

[2]From the poem "Harlem" in the larger work "Montage of a Dream Deferred" by Langston Hughes: quoted in *The Langston Hughes Reader* (New York: Braziller, 1958).

[3]Dietrich Bonhoeffer, *The Cost of Discipleship* (New York: Touchstone, 1995), 57–58.

[4]Jacob Heilbrunn, "Can Leadership Be Studied?" *Wilson Quarterly* 18, no. 2 (Spring 1994), 67.

[5]Ibid.

Chapter Six: It's a Personal Thing

[1]C. Blendinger, "Disciple," in *The New International Dictionary of New Testament Theology*, ed. Colin Brown, vol. 1 (Grand Rapids: Zondervan, 1978), 481.

[2]St. Augustine, Sermon #48, Micah 6:8.

[3]Jack Kuhatschek, *The Superman Syndrome: Finding God's Strength Where You Least Expect It* (Grand Rapids: Zondervan, 1995), 149.

[4]C. S. Lewis, *Mere Christianity* (New York: Macmillan, 1943), 174.

Chapter Seven: Radical Reformation

[1]John Leo, *U.S. News & World Report*, 21 March 1994, 22. Copyright © March 21, 1994, *U.S. News & World Report*. Used by permission.

[2]The story of Armitage Baptist Church is adapted from Joseph M. Stowell, *Overcoming Evil with Good: The Impact of a Life Well-Lived* (Chicago: Moody Press, 1995). Used with permission.

[3]Jacob Heilbrunn, "Can Leadership Be Studied?" *Wilson Quarterly* 18, no. 2 (Spring 1994), 70.

[4]Ibid.

[5]Paul Harvey, "The Day Philip Joined the Group," in *Stories for the Heart*, compiled by Alice Gray (Gresham, Oreg.: Vision House, 1996), 17–18. Used by permission of Paul Harvey.

[6]Robert Kelley, *The Power of Followership* (New York: Doubleday, 1992), 9.

[7]C. Blendinger, "Disciple," in *The New International Dictionary of New Testament Theology*, ed. Colin Brown, vol. 1 (Grand Rapids: Zondervan, 1978), 481.

[8]Peggy Noonan, "You'd Cry Too," *Forbes*, 14 September 1992, 65.

[9]C. S. Lewis, *Mere Christianity* (New York: Macmillan, 1943), 118.

Chapter Nine: Netlessness

[1]Ruth A. Tucker, *From Jerusalem to Irian Jaya* (Grand Rapids: Zondervan, 1983), 364.

²This story is adapted from Tucker, *From Jerusalem to Irian Jaya*, 363–67. Copyright © 1983 by The Zondervan Corporation. Used by permission of Zondervan Publishing House.

³Bill Hybels, "Preaching for Commitment," *Leadership Journal* 10, no. 3 (Summer 1989), 35.

Chapter Ten: Getting Out of the Way

¹The story of Dostoevsky is adapted from Joseph M. Stowell, *The Dawn's Early Light* (Chicago: Moody Press: 1990). Used with permission.

²H. Schonweiss, *"epithymia,"* in *The New International Dictionary of New Testament Theology*, ed. Colin Brown, vol. 1 (Grand Rapids: Zondervan, 1978), 456–58.

³"Troubled Waters," *Newsweek*, 26 July 1993, 21.

⁴Daniel Goleman, *Emotional Intelligence* (New York: Bantam Books, 1995), 56.

Chapter Eleven: Following as One

¹Based on a message at a Promise Keepers clergy conference in Atlanta in February 1996.

²Philip Yancey, "Why I Don't Go to a Megachurch," *Christianity Today*, May 20, 1996, 80.

³Clarence Shuler, "Reaching Beyond Barriers," *Life & Work Directions: Bible Studies for Early Adulthood*, vol. 2, no. 3 (April-May-June 1996), 7.

Chapter Twelve: Followers Are Blenders

¹Francis A. Schaeffer, *The Mark of the Christian* (Downers Grove, Ill.: InterVarsity Press, 1970).

Chapter Thirteen: Cross-Bearing

¹J. I. Packer, *Hot Tub Religion: Christian Living in a Materialistic World* (Wheaton, Ill.: Tyndale House, 1987), introduction.

²Dietrich Bonhoeffer, *The Cost of Discipleship* (New York: Touchstone, 1995), 88.

³Ibid., 89.

⁴Ibid., 88.

⁵This account and the subsequent persecution accounts are taken from papers prepared for the Moody Bible Institute's 1996 Founder's Week conference.

⁶Mrs. Howard Taylor, *The Triumph of John and Betty Stam* (Philadelphia: China Inland Mission, 1960), 102.

⁷From the play *For This Cause: The Ministry and Martyrdom of John and Betty Stam* by David H. Robey. Copyright © 1988 by David H. Robey.

⁸Adapted from Ruth A. Tucker, *From Jerusalem to Irian Jaya* (Grand Rapids: Zondervan, 1983), 422–23. Copyright © 1983 by The Zondervan Corporation. Used by permission of Zondervan Publishing House.

We want to hear from you. Please send your comments about this book to us in care of the address below. Thank you.

ZondervanPublishingHouse
Grand Rapids, Michigan 49530
http://www.zondervan.com